What people are saying about

Pagan Portals...

In her wonderful book, *Pagan* ....rgan Daimler takes us into the mystical mythol ..... . Lugh as the many-skilled king and warrior of the Tuatha De Danann. She takes us back into history and brings forth this fascinating god of the Irish Celts into a modern understanding of him. This book is highly recommended to anyone who seeks to reach into the depths of the Irish Otherworld.

Chris Allaun, author of *Otherworld: Ecstatic Witchcraft for the Spirits of the Land* and *Upperworld: Shamanism and Magick of the Celestial Realm*

As a longtime devotee of Lugh and fan of Morgan Daimler's work, I am delighted to recommend her latest book, this time on the omni-talented god, Lugh. With his origins in oaths, skills, and storms; Morgan Daimler, speaking cogently to his nature, and how he has been perceived over time, once again demonstrates her expertise and familiarity with the material, in the concise, thorough, accurate, and accessible way that has become hallmark of her style. For those who are trying to get to know the sometimes difficult to grasp, but important god, Lugh, and for those already familiar with him, Morgan Daimler's latest work will be a worthwhile addition to your library.

Brian Walsh, Storyteller, Therapist, Chaplain and author of *The Secret Commonwealth and the Fairy Belief Complex*

Well researched, providing a concise source book of pretty much everything you could possibly want to know about Lugh.

Luke Eastwood, author of *The Druid's Primer*

Well researched and clearly written, Morgan Daimler provides another concise and essential guide to one of our most beloved Celtic deities. Highly recommended.
Danu Forest, Celtic scholar and author of *Wild Magic - Celtic folk traditions for the solitary practitioner*

At the heart of Morgan Daimler's text is the transition between how Lugh was portrayed in Irish myth and folklore, and how that was changed, particularly in the early 20th Century. The differences are quite startling, but Daimler takes the reader through these differences with confidence and authority. There is plenty of scope for the reader to begin their own investigation of Lugh, with an interesting array of resources referenced throughout. This is the perfect re-introduction to a well-known God who may not be who you thought he was!
Andrew Anderson, author of *The Ritual of Writing* and *Artio and Artaois*

Pagan Portals
Lugh

Meeting the Many-skilled God

Pagan Portals

Lugh

Meeting the Many-skilled God

Morgan Daimler

MOON
BOOKS

Winchester, UK
Washington, USA

JOHN HUNT PUBLISHING

First published by Moon Books, 2021
Moon Books is an imprint of John Hunt Publishing Ltd., No. 3 East Street, Alresford
Hampshire SO24 9EE, UK
office@jhpbooks.net
www.johnhuntpublishing.com
www.moon-books.net

For distributor details and how to order please visit the 'Ordering' section on our website.

Text copyright: Morgan Daimler 2020

ISBN: 978 1 78904 428 7
978 1 78904 429 4 (ebook)
Library of Congress Control Number: 2020939090

All rights reserved. Except for brief quotations in critical articles or reviews, no part of this
book may be reproduced in any manner without prior written permission from the publishers.

The rights of Morgan Daimler as author have been asserted in accordance with the Copyright,
Designs and Patents Act 1988.

A CIP catalogue record for this book is available from the British Library.

Design: Stuart Davies

UK: Printed and bound by CPI Group (UK) Ltd, Croydon, CR0 4YY
Printed in North America by CPI GPS partners

We operate a distinctive and ethical publishing philosophy in
all areas of our business, from our global network of authors to
production and worldwide distribution.

Contents

Other Titles by Morgan Daimler

The Morrigan
Meeting the Great Queens
978-1-78279-833-0 (Paperback)
978-1-78279-834-7 (e-book)

Brigid
Meeting the Celtic Goddess of Poetry, Forge, and Healing Well
978-1-78535-320-8 (Paperback)
978-1-78535-321-5 (e-book)

Manannán mac Lir
Meeting the Celtic God of Wave and Wonder
978-1-78535-810-4 (Paperback)
978-1-78535-811-1 (e-book)

The Dagda
Meeting the Good God of Ireland
978-1-78535-640-7 (Paperback)
978-1-78535-641-4 (e-book)

Irish Paganism
Reconstructing Irish Polytheism
978-1-78535-145-7 (Paperback)
978-1-78535-146-4 (e-book)

Gods and Goddesses of Ireland
A Guide to Irish Deities
978-1-78279-315-1 (Paperback)
978-1-78535-450-2 (e-book)

A New Dictionary of Fairies
*A 21st Century Exploration of Celtic and Related Western
European Fairies*
978-1-78904-036-4 (paperback)
978-1-78904-037-1 (e-book)

Fairies
A Guide to the Celtic Fair Folk
978-1-78279-650-3 (paperback)
978-1-78279-696-1 (e-book)

Fairycraft
Following the Path of Fairy Witchcraft
978-1-78535-051-1 (paperback)
978-1-78535-052-8 (e-book)

Fairy Queens
Meeting the Queens of the Otherworld
978-1-78535-833-3 (paperback)
978-1-78535-842-5 (e-book)

Fairy Witchcraft
A Neopagan's Guide to the Celtic Fairy Faith
978-1-78279-343-4 (paperback)
978-1-78279-344-1 (e-book)

Travelling the Fairy Path
Experiencing the myth, magic, and mysticism of Fairy Witchcraft
978-1-78535-752-7 (paperback)
978-1-78535-753-4 (e-book)

Thor
Untangling older beliefs from modern popculture
978-1-78904-115-6 (Paperback)
978-1-78904-116-3 (e-book)

Odin
Meeting the Norse Allfather
978-1-78535-480-9 (Paperback)
978-1-78535-481-6 (e-book)

Where the Hawthorn Grows
An American Druid's reflections
978-1-78099-969-2 (Paperback)
978-1-78099-968-5 (e-book)

This book is for all who follow the Many-Gifted God
in the world today and all who are seeking him.

Dedicated to the memory of Cori Taylor, a woman of many
skills and a generous spirit who will be greatly missed by
everyone who knew and loved her.

Acknowledgements

A huge thank you to everyone who offered modern media examples of Lugh in fiction and games. Jennifer, Corey, Tania, Bridget, Amy, Patti, Patricia, Carla, Jenna, Echo, Parker, Brandy, Mel, Jenna, and Chad I deeply appreciate the examples you all shared.

Special thanks to Brian Walsh for constructive criticism on the draft of this book.

Author's Note

Irish paganism has been steadily gaining in popularity and while more attention tends to be paid to the goddesses, there are several higher profile gods including Lugh. Despite this general popularity it can be surprisingly difficult to find good sources about him because he is often only discussed shallowly or conflated with various counterparts from other Celtic language cultures. The same basic information about him is repeated from source to source, often freely mixing older mythology with modern opinions. Because of this *Pagan Portals - Lugh* was written as a resource for seekers of the Irish god of many skills based on both solid academic material, older mythology, folklore, and modern anecdotes. It is meant to be a basic introduction to this deity and also a bridge for beginners to feel more comfortable as they seek to learn more about this powerful and important deity before moving forward.

In writing this I have drawn on many different sources and have carefully referenced and cited all of them. My own degree is in psychology so I prefer to use the APA method of citations. This means that within the text after quotes or paraphrased material the reader will see a set of parenthesis containing the author's last name and date the source was published; this can then be cross references with the bibliography at the end of the book. I find this method to be a good one and I prefer it over footnotes or other methods of citation which is why it's the one I use. I have also included end notes in some places where a point needs to be expanded on or further discussed but where it would be awkward to do that within the text itself.

I would also like to add a note here about the spelling throughout this book. I include the names in the original languages as much as possible and prefer to avoid Anglicization wherever possible, however prior to the 20th century there was no standardized spelling in Irish and the Irish language itself features grammatical forms not found in English, which means that there are variations in how the names are spelled that I realize may be confusing to English speakers. I will try to use one main spelling for each primary name as much as possible except when quoting a source that uses a variant spelling. While this book can and does serve as a stand-alone work, ideally, I hope that the reader will be drawn to learn more and decide to continue seeking. Lugh is a multi-layered deity and it would take a book of a much greater length to cover all of his complexity. That is why this text is meant as an introduction and not a definitive guide. In order for readers to use this book as a stepping stone towards further research I have provided a list of both the references I used in my writing and also of recommended further reading at the end of the book under the bibliography. I have tried to offer books which represent an array of options for people, with different viewpoints and approaches to honouring Lugh. I would note, however, that as far as I know at the time I am writing this, there is no other full-length nonfiction book written only on Lugh. Most readers who are seeking to learn more about Lugh will need to research the original myths for themselves as well as looking for what material can be found piecemeal in more modern books on Irish or Celtic paganism. I highly recommend looking at the original mythology to get a feel for Lugh's personality.

As I have said before in my previous *Pagan Portals*, I do not think that the religious framework we use to connect to the Gods matters as much as the effort to honour the old Gods itself. I think we can all do this respectfully and with an appreciation for history without the need for any particular religion. Whether we are Reconstructionists, Wiccans, or Celtic pagans all that really matter is that we are approaching our faith with sincerity and a genuine intention. To that end this book is written without any specific spiritual faith in mind, beyond polytheism, and it is up to the reader to decide how best to incorporate the material. My own personal path is rooted in witchcraft and reconstruction so that is bound to colour some of my opinions in the text, however, so the reader may want to keep that in mind.

I have been an Irish pagan since 1991 and have long had a deep respect for Lugh although I do not have a strong personal connection to him. He is not one of the primary Gods I honour but he is an important deity within the Tuatha De Danann and I think that to understand the Irish Gods one must have at least a basic understanding of Lugh and his wider role. For some people this book may be the first step towards connecting to this important deity. For others this book may simply provide a greater understanding of Lugh, his history, and modern beliefs and practices associated with him. In either case I hope that the reader feels that some value is gained from the time spent with this little volume, getting to know Lugh.

Introduction

One of the most popular of the Irish Gods is Lugh, known as Lug in older Irish and Lú in modern Irish. His name has multiple variants in older Irish including Luch, Lucc, Luog, Lugo, Lugai, and Lochca (Grey, 1983). He features heavily in some of the most important mythology of the Tuatha De Danann and appears in more subtle ways in in other myths, including the Táin Bó Cúailnge. He is also a pan-Celtic deity who can be found in other Celtic language speaking cultures, notably the Welsh and Gaulish.

The name Lugh is derived from the proto-Indo-European root *leug(h) which most likely means 'to swear an oath' (O hOgain, 2006). The meaning of Lugh's name has been heavily debated for many years however and while the oath-taking meaning can be strongly supported there are other options, such as 'light', that one will find reading through articles about him. I'd encourage readers to keep the oath-taking meaning in mind but consider the alternate meanings suggested as a sort of folk etymology, reflecting perceptions of Lugh.

There are arguments put forth that Lugh and his Welsh counterpart Lleu were late arrivals to insular Celtic belief, having been imported from the continent. This pattern of deity spread and importation is not uncommon and can be seen with other deities who do have firmer suggested arrival dates; there is no such arrival date with Lugh or clear pattern of transmission[1]. In contrast Koch suggests that Lugh wasn't a later graft into the Tuatha De Danann but rather *arrives late on the scene in myth because he is the god of advanced culture* (Koch, 1992, p 253, footnote 22). Whether or not Lugh was an early arrival or later import his importance within Irish Celtic belief is clear and there are at least two earlier Irish tribal groups who took their names from Lugh. The Luigni – literally people of Lugh - in Connacht and the Luigni Temro [people of Lugh of Teamhair] in county Meath, groups who can be attested back to the 4th or 5th century through Ogham inscriptions on stones (Williams, 2016).

Another sign of Lugh's importance is the number of personal names associated with him, including the popular Lugaid and Lugadech, which likely mean something close to 'person who honours Lugh'. There is some debate about whether the 'lu' part of the name here refers to the deity or is the later Irish word for a warrior or hero, but since the later term is likely based in the name of the deity and referring to him, however obliquely later, the connection between the name and Lugh still stands (Williams, 2016). We find similar names in Britain and Gaul, via inscriptions, which also may reflect[2] a connection to the deity in his various cultural iterations.

Lugh is a complex figure, both inside Ireland and in related cultures. His widespread popularity across various regions and the collected mythology has created a patchwork of stories and beliefs that may contradict each other or seem incompatible yet which all reflect genuine beliefs. All of the material that can feasibly be presented in this text will be and the contradictions will be dealt with whenever possible but the reader should be aware that where Lugh is involved there may not be easy or straightforward answers. He can be found in forms that are clearly divine in nature, such as Lugh of the Tuatha De Danann, but also appears acting in a divine manner in stories where he declares himself *"of the seed of Adam"*[3] and later further euhemerized into a human form as the founder of septs or teacher of human kings.

Understanding Lugh, ultimately, is about accepting all of these contradictions rather than trying to find answers to them. Lugh's complexity cannot be simplified but that doesn't prevent us from creating a single image of him from the pieces that we have to work with. As you read on, do so with an open mind and a willingness to consider the multitude of correct answers to single questions and you will find yourself beginning, I think, to understand who Lugh is.

End Notes

1 Brighid would be a good example of such importation and transmission as there are firmer theories about her migrations and which groups carried her to new areas. I discuss this in my previous work *Pagan Portals - Brigid*.

2 There has also been some suggestion that the names referencing lugos for warriors may actually be using a homonym meaning lynx, although John Carey has argued strongly against that interpretation. Further on this can be found in Williams book 'Ireland's Immortals' and Carey's article 'Celtic Lugus 'Lynx': A Phantom Big Cat?'

3 Quoting the Baile an Scáil, where Lugh appears to the human king Conn in the Otherworld to convey sovereignty and a prophecy to him, but begins by telling Conn that Lugh is human, dead, and a revered ancestor.

Chapter 1

Who is Lugh?

"After the death of Nuadu and of those men, Lug took the kingship of Ireland, and his grandfather Balar the Strong-smiter fell at his hands, with a stone from his sling. Lugh was forty years in the kingship of Ireland after the last battle of Mag Tuired"
Macalister, 1944

Lugh is a popular character in Irish mythology and was understood to be a popular God during the pagan period. He was depicted as both heroic and tempestuous, skilled and hot tempered, an excellent king and also sometimes unforgiving. He is compared to Biblical figures like King David and the archangel Michael and appears as a pagan figure with the virtues valued by monotheism, yet he is also solidly depicted as a pagan deity and member of the Otherworldly Tuatha De Danann. All of these contradictions exist within the character of Lugh who has been shaped across millennia of shifting culture. He was never a sun God yet he is a sun god to many people today. He is still known as a great warrior yet his role as a mediator of sovereignty is not often discussed anymore. To understand who Lugh was and is and may yet become we must begin with his main features and relations.

Lugh was one of the High Kings of the Tuatha Dé Danann, ruling for 40 years after Nuada, and he was the only one who could defeat his grandfather, the Fomorian Balor, in the second Battle of Maige Tuired, placing him in a pivotal position in the mythology. During this battle we see Lugh demonstrating his epithet of many-skilled as he earns his way into the High King's hall by proving he has more skills than any other single individual among the Gods. Before the battle itself we also see him actively using his magical skill to rally his army and to curse the opposing army (Gray, 1983). This multitude of skills, including magical ability, is a core facet of Lugh's nature and perhaps reflects the source of his wider appeal as he was a deity who resonated with people across social dynamics, a god of kings and also of skilled labourers, of poets and magicians, of warriors and healers.

Lugh's adeptness with all skills that were valued among the nobility is one of his key characteristics. He contains within himself all of the skills of his civilization, and in doing so he outshines the reigning king Nuada who has no such excessive talent (Williams, 2016). When he first arrives at the royal court of the Tuatha De Danann he is challenged before being allowed in and offers a series of skills that he can perform including as a builder, smith, champion, harper, warrior, poet, historian, sorcerer, physician, cupbearer, and brazier. He later goes on to prove his cleverness by defeating all present in a game of fidchell[1], his strength by matching the champion Ogma's throw of a heavy flagstone, and his skill with the harp by playing the three traditional strains of music[2]. Two of his epithets are based around his many skills and his role as the superlative leader and deity is often predicated on his vast knowledge and ability.

He is also in many ways the ideal king in contrast to Bres mac Elatha and may, therefore, have symbolized the importance of patrilineal inheritance. Bres is the son of a Fomorian father and Tuatha De Danann mother; Lugh represents the inverse of this as the son of a Tuatha De Danann father and Fomorian mother. When Nuada is maimed in the Cét-Cath Maige Tuired and loses his kingship afterwards it is the women of the Tuatha De Danann who urge the group to accept Bres as their new king. Bres proves to be a poor king and allows his paternal kin to put the Tuatha De Danann under great oppression. In contrast Lugh shows up in their greatest hour of need and proves himself skilled in every craft and noble skill, motivating King Nuada to voluntarily step aside and let Lugh lead the Tuatha De Danann into battle. While the idea of the two figures representing juxtaposing values of kinship may seem to be a foreign or even offensive concept to modern thinkers, it does reflect the mindset of the times that the stories were recorded in. This implicit bias must always be considered and whether we agree with the underlying viewpoint or not there is value in exploring the way it may have shaped aspects of the mythology.

Lugh's place as the idealized king may have been so deeply ingrained that even after the conversion to Christianity he was retained as a symbol of divine sovereignty. Williams suggest this as an explanation for Lugh's retention as both a literary figure and euhemerized human ancestor, as well as the persistence of the idea that Lugh was incarnating as or favouring human heroes who bore his name (Williams, 2016). In this way Lugh becomes a contrasting figure to the divine Christ and Christian God, having both echoes of their stories worked into his own but also being used perhaps to show the lesser power of the pagan gods; for example Williams posits that Cu Chulainn's triple conception may have been a subtle commentary on the pagan god's inability to easily do what the Christian god had, that is conceive a mortal child or incarnate in a mortal form. While this would obviously reflect a much later bias being written into the material by Christian scholars it also demonstrates the continued importance and power of Lugh, that even hundreds of years after conversion there was both a need to bring Lugh down and also an understanding of his continued importance.

One final less emphasized but still vital aspect to Lugh is his appearance in a later text as a Scál. This word, like many in older Irish, is difficult to translate because it has many layers of meaning including ghost, phantom, spirit, hero, champion, giant, and person. MacNeill, citing another author, suggests that it may best be applied *"to disembodied spirits of the dead or supernatural beings"* (MacNeill, 1962, p 6). Lugh appears as such a being to the king Conn and Lugh's father is called 'Scál Balb' in the Lebor Gabala Erenn. This may have been one way that Lugh remained active and relevant after the conversion period, losing his explicit divinity but remaining a clearly powerful and important supernatural being that could not easily be fit into the more common categories of saints or demons that were the fate of other members of the Tuatha De Danann.

Lugh's Epithets

Lugh is given several epithets including Lamhfada [long arm], Ildanach[3] [many skilled], and Samildanach [many joined skills]. Lamhfada is a reference to his skill with the sling, and possibly spear, not of physically long arms. Ildanach and Samildanach are both clear references to the wide variety of skills he has mastered and can demonstrate.

He is also sometimes called either Mac Céin, son of Cian, or Mac Ethlenn, son of Eithne (MacKillop, 1998). The use of both his patronymic and matronymic throughout the source material is very interesting and somewhat unusual as both humans and gods were usually only called consistently by one or the other.

One of the epithets applied to him in the Lebor Gabala Erenn is 'rind-agach' which Macalister gives as 'spear slaughterous' (Macalister, 1944). I believe 'spear combative' is a closer translation of rind-agach and also fits with Lugh's personality which is, indeed, combative.

He may also occasionally be referred to as Maicnia (MacKillop, 1998). This may be read as 'young warrior' or 'youthful hero'. A more obscure epithet it could be a reference to Lugh's relative youth in the Cath Maige Tuired or a way to emphasize his place in contrast to deities like Nuada and the Dagda.

In the Cath Maige Tuired when arriving at Teamhair he introduces himself as Lug Lonnansclech; there is no clear translation of this term but I would suggest habitually-fierce or unchangeably fierce[4]. Later in the Cath Maige Tuired when talking with the Fomorian poet Loch Leathglas Lugh calls himself 'Lug Lonnbemnech' and Loch refers to him as 'Lugh Leathsuanaigh' (Gray, 1983). Lonnbemnech means fierce-smiting or strong cutting. Leathsuanaigh can be understood as half-foxglove-red, if we interpret it as leath – half and sianach – foxglove-coloured, and is explained in a gloss on the text which says that such a reddish colour was on Lugh from sunset to sunrise (Gray, 1983). Later medieval literati would seek to explain leathsuanaigh (alternately spelled leathshuanach) by seeing it as leath – half and suan – cloaked and saying that he had a particular red-gold shirt (O hOgain, 2006; MacNeill, 1962). Possible related to this second interpretation Lugh was also sometimes called Lugh Na Leind, or Lugh of the mantles.

Lugh's Appearance

Irish mythology is often short on descriptive details even of significant figures. When we see Lugh being discussed it is mostly in terms of his skill rather than his personal appearance, for example the Lebor Gabala Erenn calls him *"a cliff without wrinkle"* to describe his perfection (Macalister. 1944) Nonetheless we do have a few hints about how Lugh would look in a human form.

In the Cath Maige Tuired Lugh is described as *"[a] handsome, well built young warrior with a king's diadem"* (Gray, 1983).

The first recension of the Táin Bó Cúailnge describes Lugh this way:

"A man fair and tall, with a great head of curly yellow hair. He has a green mantle wrapped about him and a brooch of white silver in the mantle over his breast. Neat to his white skin he wears a tunic of royal satin with red-gold insertion reaching to his knees. He carries a black shield with a hard boss of white-bronze. In his hand a five-pointed spear and next to it a forked javelin." (O'Rahilly, 1976)

Although less detailed in its description the Baile an Scáil describes him this way: "*There was never in Tara a man of his size or his beauty, on account of the fairness of his form and the wondrousness of his appearance.*" (Dillon, 1946).

From this we can perhaps conclude that Lugh when in a human seeming would appear as a handsome younger man with an athletic build and curly blond hair.

Relationships

As with many things in Irish mythology there are often contradiction to be found when looking at the genealogy of deities. Here I'll present the most common version of Lugh's parentage and relationships and then discuss other options given in various sources. Some of this will be repeated in the sections below as we try to untangle the material. While this repetition may feel unnecessary, I believe it is the best way for a reader unfamiliar with the names and ideas presented to learn and retain them. Impatient readers may skip the following sections if they prefer.

According to the Cath Maige Tuired which details Lugh's later arrival among the Tuatha De Danann, Lugh was the son of the De Danann Cian and the Fomorian Eithne; his paternal grandfather was the physician God, Dian Cécht and his maternal grandfather the dangerous Fomorian Balor who had an evil eye that could kill anyone it looked on. Arriving at Teamhair Lugh states this ancestry and that he was fostered by the Fir Bolg woman Tailtiu and Eochaid Garb mac Dúach [rough Eochaid son of Dúach]. According to the Lebor Gabala Erenn Eochaid Garb was a man of the Tuatha De Danann, and Tailtiu's second husband after her first, the Fir Bolg king Eochaid mac Erc, was killed. Tailtiu as Lugh's foster mother and Cian son of Dian Cecht as his father is supported by the various existing versions of the Lebor Gabala Erenn as well as the previously mentioned Cath Maige Tuired.

Alternately the Cét-Cath Maige Tuired, Acallamh na Senorach, and Oidheadh Chloinne Tuireann say that Lugh's father was Cían[5] whose father was Cáinte, and gives Cian's two brothers as Cu and Ceithin. Lugh's Fomorian mother Ethniu remains the same although some sources spell her name Ethliu and Lugh is said to be one of seven sons she had (Grey, 1983). In likewise while Tailtiu is often said to be his foster mother, Manannán is elsewhere named as his foster father and in a later section of the Cath Maige Tuired it is claimed that Lugh had nine foster fathers: Tollusdam, Echdam, Eru, Rechtaid Finn, Fosad, Feidlimid, Ibar, Scibar, and Minn. Some sources even list Goibhniu as a possible foster father for Lugh (MacKillop, 1998).

I realize this is confusing and contradictory and the source material offers no clarity. I would suggest that the variations between his father and his foster parents likely represent various local folk traditions that were later brought into regional and then popular texts. Rather than seeking one definitive view or understanding we should instead appreciate the variety that is presented and see all of this as true in relation to Lugh no matter how contradictory the various pieces may seem.

Lugh may have been a triplet with two unnamed brothers. According to several versions of Lugh's birth story there was a prophecy that Balor's grandson would kill him so Balor imprisoned his daughter in a tower; Cian snuck in and had a tryst with Eithne which resulted in triplets. When Balor found the babies, he cast them into the sea where two of them either drowned or were turned into seals, while Lugh was saved by either Manannán or Birog. Lugh was then fostered by either Manannán or Tailtiu (MacKillop, 1998). One version of the story says that the Tuatha De Danann druidess Birog aided Cian to meet Ethniu while another says it was Manannán who helped Cian to accomplish this task, as part of a wider scheme to get a magical cow from Balor. By that account Cian fathered Lugh and also successfully escaped Balor's island with the baby, however he gave him over to Manannán to foster. And of course, there is yet another alternate story in the Cath Maige Tuired which says that Ethniu and Cian were paired intentionally to gain peace between the Fomorians and Tuatha De Danann (Gray, 1983; O hOgain, 2006). Lugh might also have a sister named Ebliu. She is an obscure figure connected to the area around Munster, who was said to be married to Fintan Mac Bochra (MacKillop, 1998).

In myth and folklore Lugh is given four different wives: Buí or Búa (possibly also known as the Cailleach Bhéirre), Nás, Echtach, and Englic (MacKillop, 1998). Another source mentions Lugh having a wife named Búach, possibly identical to Buí/Búa, although this Búach is specified as the daughter of Daire Donn (Grey, 1983). One of these wives was unfaithful and had an affair with the Dagda's son Cermait, prompting Lugh's vengeful killing of him; according to one source the wife in question was Englic while another claims it was Búach (Grey, 1983). This murder in turn eventually led the three sons of Cermait to seek revenge on Lugh for their father's death.

In the Ulster cycle he is said to be the father of the hero Cu Chulainn by the mortal woman Deichtire although Cu Chulainn does simultaneously have a mortal father as well. This is achieved through a series of strange events and multiple conceptions/births/and-or deaths of the child before he is finally born as Setanta, later to be known as Cu Chulainn. We see Lugh coming to Cu Chulainn's aid in the Tain Bo Cuiligne, declaring himself Cu Chulainn's father, and when the hero is gravely injured Lugh acts in a decidedly fatherly role, healing Cu Chulainn and taking his place in the battle.

The multiple conceptions and births of Setanta have led to various, sometimes complex, theories about Lugh's ultimate connection to the resulting child including the idea that the child could have been an avatar for Lugh himself. While I am personally sceptical of that since we see Lugh as himself coming to Cu Chulainn's aid it is possible that this apparent contradiction would not have been seen as such by the original audience. As John Waddell puts it in *'Archaeology and Celtic Myth'*:

"A medieval audience would not have seen anything implausible or incongruous here, for the symbolic significance and societal implications of various details and the apparent contradictions would have alerted them to deeper meanings and resonated in ways that we can only dimly comprehend" (Waddell, 2014, page13).

The Rennes Dindshenchas mentions Lugh having a son named Ainle. In the Fenian cycle Fionn's poet Cnú Deireóil claims to be Lugh's son, although this may be more hyperbole than literal (MacKillop, 1998). There are also several human family lines and septs that claimed descent from human versions or incarnations of Lugh.

Lugh also had several members among the Tuatha De Danann that he had less than friendly relationships with. He defeated Bres after the battle of Maige Tuired and although Bres's life was spared Lugh would later kill him. As mentioned above Lugh killed Cermait mac Dagda for cuckolding him with one of Lugh's wives; Cermait was later brought back to life by the Dagda and it isn't hard to imagine the two deities didn't get on well. The three sons of Cermait kill Lugh so they clearly had enmity between them. There are also hints in some of the stories that Lugh and Nuada, who preceded Lugh as king of the Tuatha De, had at best an uneasy relationship (Grey, 1983).

Lugh's Family

I realize the above section is a lot of information, much of it confusing. I will recap it here in a different format to help people struggling to conceptualize Lugh's connections to various other beings.

Cian – the son of Dian Cecht, Cian is Lugh's father in several of the primary sources. He snuck onto Balor's island, with assistance from either Manannan or Birog, and had a tryst with Balor's daughter Ethniu, resulting in Lugh. Cian was transformed by magic into a pig as a baby and would retain the ability to take this shape throughout his life (MacKillop, 1998). He would die at the hands of the three sons of Tuireann just before the Cath Maige Tuired.

Cían – alternately his father may have been Cían son of Cáinte, a different personage from the above Cian. This Cían is a more obscure figure.

Ethniu – the daughter or the Fomorian king Balor of the evil-eye, Ethniu was kept on an island in a keep with only women for companionship to prevent a prophecy that her son would kill her father. Despite this she bore a child to the Tuatha De Danann Cian (or Cían).

Balor – Lugh's grandfather is the Fomorian king Balor, a fierce and dangerous being who has a poisonous eye which, according to the Cath Maige Tuired, paralyzes or stuns any who it looks upon. Because of this eye is kept closed except in battle when the lid is lifted by four people who pull it up by means of a ring through the eye lid.

Dian Cecht – the premier physician of the Tuatha De Danann he is Lugh's grandfather. Dian Cecht was a prolific being with many children including the other physician deities Airmed, Miach, Ormiach, and Ochtriuil, as well as Cu, Cethan, and Lugh's father Cian, and Etan the poetess.

Tailtiu – Lugh's foster mother is Tailtiu who is said to be the daughter of Magmór [literally great plain] king of Spain. In spite of this pseudo-historical connection to Europe Tailtiu is generally understood to be one of the Fir Bolg. She may be a reflection of an older pre-Celtic deity in Ireland (MacKillop, 1998).

Manannán – In some texts Manannán, rather than Tailtiu, is the one who fosters Lugh after helping Cian to engage in an affair with Ethniu (and escape afterwards). By these accounts he raises Lugh with him on Emhain Abhlac, which is one explanation for why Lugh does not arrive among the Tuatha De Danann until significantly later.

Goibhniu, Credne, and Luchte – the three gods of skill – smith, wright, and carpenter – were Lugh's paternal great-uncles according to the Lebor Gabala Erenn because they are Dian Cecht's brothers. Goibhniu is also mentioned as another possible foster father to Lugh (MacKillop, 1998).

Cu Chulainn – Cu Chulainn is one of the more complicated figures within Irish mythology, and while he is often understood as a human character or heroic figure he may best be described as a demi-god. His conception is a convoluted affair and while he is seen as the son of Lugh, he is also considered to have a mortal father, his mother's husband Sultam. Despite this overlapping mortal parentage Lugh aids Cu Chulainn during the Táin Bó Cúailnge and seems to have a vested interest in his partially human offspring.

Wives

Lugh has four wives according to mythology although we do not have a lot of information about these women nor do we know if these marriages were simultaneous or individual. There is also a reference to a fifth named wife, who may or may not be a conflation of one of the previous ones. These wives were briefly mentioned above but in this section, we will look at each in a bit more depth where possible.

Buí – sister to Nás according to the Metrical Dindshenchas, Buí is said to be buried at Cnogba [Knowth] which is named for her. The Dindshenchas say that Bui was the daughter of Ruadri [red king] who is called the king of Britain and she is referred to as 'Bui of the battles' (Gwyn, 1913).

It is probable that this Buí is also known as the Cailleach Bhéara. O hOgain gives the Cailleach Bhéara's name as Boí while the early Irish poem The Lament of the Old Woman of Beara says *"Is mé Caillech Bérri, Buí"* [I am the Cailleach Bheara, Buí]

(O hOgain, 2006; Murphy, 1956). O Cathasaigh agrees with this suggestion in his article 'The Eponym of Cnogba' where he cites O'Rahilly as the original source of the idea but then goes on to defend it successfully and to connect the Cailleach to Buí and to Cnogba. Waddell doesn't connect Buí directly to the Cailleach but does suggest that she is a sovereignty goddess and that her burial place may have been an entrance to Emhain Abhlac.

Nás – sister to Bui and another daughter of Ruadri. She is one of Lugh's wives and is said to be the mother of a son named Ibic; no father is named for this child. Nás would have a Lughnasa festival held for her at the location named for her, instituted by Lugh after her death.

Echtach – an obscure figure that we do not have much information on.

Englic – according to some sources, including Gray, Englic was one of Lugh's wives although the Metrical Dindshenchas tells us that Oengus mac ind Og was in love with her and Midhir kidnapped her at one point. This may have been the wife who had the affair with Cermait mac Dagda.

Búach – the daughter of Daire Donn, by some accounts the wife who had an affair with Cermait. Búach may or may not be identical to Buí

End Notes

1   Fidchell is a board game of strategy somewhat like chess.

2   In many Irish tales these three types of music are mentioned, with mastery of all being a true sign of skill. They are: sleep music, sorrowful music, and joyful music. When a master plays each one the correlating effect should occur among the listeners so that sleep music puts the audience to sleep and sad music makes them weep or happy music makes them dance.

3   Gray points out in her notes in the Cath Maige Tuired that Il-ildánach is used for emphasis of skill and was used by

Keating to indicate craft heads.

4 Lonnansclech – possibly from lonn – fierce and clech – habitually or ansclithe/anscuithe – unchangeable.

5 To further add to this confusion Cian may also be known as Cethren, and several of the mortal heroes thought to be versions of Lugh have a father named Dáire, causing MacKillop to suggest that Dáire may also be an alternate name for Cian. The Lebor Gabala Erenn says that Cian is also called Scál Balb, silent spirit/hero.

Chapter 2

Lugh in Irish Myth and Folklore

"Lugh was heartening the men of Ireland that they should fight the battle fervently so that they should not be any longer in bondage. For it was better for them to find death in protecting their fatherland than to bide under bondage and tribute as they had been. Wherefore then Lugh sang this chant below, as he went round the men of Erin, on one foot and with one eye closed"
(Stokes, 1891)

It is not surprising that Lugh is to be found across an array of mythology and folklore. He is certainly not the only significant god among the Tuatha De Danann but he does seem to hold a special place in the narratives, something that is reflected perhaps by his continued importance in the later folklore. Lugh is the young king who comes in to displace the older one, his exceptional skill exceeding all others except perhaps the Dagda[1], Lugh's narrative includes missteps and his own death, yet who goes on despite this[2] to help father the epic hero Cu Chulainn.

In this chapter we will look at some of the most significant appearances of Lugh throughout Irish mythology and folklore, including a brief summary of each appearance and retelling of Lugh's role within that story. This should be understood as only a basic guide, with portions of the stories that do not feature Lugh omitted for brevity. As always, I encourage readers to go directly to these sources for themselves as no summary can do the full tale justice and much can be learned by seeing how the various deities are portrayed and interact in the original material. That said I do believe it's important for those seeking Lugh to understand his wider actions in the stories which is why these retellings are included.

Cath Maige Tuired – The Cath Maige Tuired is possibly the most important story featuring the Tuatha De Danann and describes one of the most pivotal moments in their mythology. There is only one surviving text that contains this tale, held now in the British Museum, although fragments of the story can also be found elsewhere and it is referenced in other mythology. The surviving manuscript is later in date but the contents of the Cath Maige Tuired have been dated to the 12th century but likely based on material dating back further to the 9th century.

Lugh is a pivotal character in the story of the Cath Maige Tuired, which tells of the Tuatha De Danann overthrowing the Fomorians who are oppressing them under the rule of the half-Fomorian, half-De Danann king Bres. The story has many aspects to it and features all of the significant members of the Tuatha De Danann in one way or another; Lugh is arguably one of the most important despite not appearing until a third of the way into the tale.

When we first meet Lugh in this story it is as he arrives at the gates of Teamhair, the seat of power for the Tuatha De Danann and site of Nuada's royal court. The doorkeeper asks who he is and he replies that he is Lugh Lonnansclech and gives his parentage on both sides. The doorkeeper challenges him, saying that he must have a skill[3] to be allowed in and Lugh goes on to list all of his abilities only to be told after each that the Tuatha De already have a person with that skill. Finally, he asks if they have any one person who can do all of the things he has claimed, then beats everyone at a board game of strategy, fidchell, after which Nuada finally allows him in. He further engages in a test of strength and accuracy against the champion Ogma and then plays the three types of music – sleep, sorrowful, and joyful - for everyone in the hall. After seeing all of this Nuada decides to switch seats[4] with Lugh and allow him to lead the Tuatha De Danann against the Fomorians, believing that Lugh has the better chance of success.

The story moves ahead about a year, and finds Lugh going with the Dagda and Ogma to the obscure three gods of Danann who equip him for the battle. After receiving this equipment, The Morrigan goes to Lugh and chants an incitement to him, encouraging him to rise up and fight fiercely and relentlessly against the Fomorians. A few weeks later, the day before Samhain [Halloween] all of the Tuatha De gathered again in preparation for the battle and Lugh sent the Dagda out to spy upon the Fomorians.

Following this the text tells us that the Tuatha De Danann had decided to keep Lugh away from the battle in order to protect him, because of his enormous talents. Nonetheless he met with the pre-eminent warriors and asked them each what they would contribute to the battel, echoing a passage earlier in the story when Nuada had done the same, but speaking to different people and getting somewhat different responses. He did this, according to the story, in order to give them strength and afterwards *"every man had the courage of a king or great lord"* (Gray, 1983, p 55).

When the battle itself was to begin, the Tuatha De left Lugh in their camp under the guard of his nine foster fathers, but he escaped disguised as a chariot warrior. He joined the rest of them before the fighting began and in one of the more important scenes of the story, he engaged in an act of battle magic. He urged his own people to fight to the death rather than live under the oppression of the Fomorians, and he circled the Tuatha De on one foot with one eye closed[5] chanting an incitement upon the armies. A great and bloody battle ensues which culminates with the death of Nuada and Macha by Balor and Lugh's confrontation of his grandfather.

In the published translations of the story the initial meeting of Balor and Lugh is not translated. It is too long for me to include a full translation here but, paraphrased, the two engage in a war of words, each promising destruction to the other. It begins with Lugh claiming that he will be Balor's death and Balor acknowledging that he knows Lugh is his grandson. Lugh then goes on to recite a battle poem against his grandfather, boasting of his own skill and promising the destruction of Balor and the Fomorians. After this untranslated section Balor asks that the lid of his poisonous eye be lifted so that he can gaze upon Lugh. As soon as the eye opens Lugh hurls a sling stone at it, driving it back through Balor's head so that is looks on his own army instead. Balor then fell on his own men, killing 27 of them and injuring the king Indech mac De Domnann. Indech then calls for his poet Loch Lethglas and asks to know who has caused this, to which Lug responds with another long speech that is not usually translated.

The Morrigan arrives and encourages the fighters and the Tuatha De Danann take the day. Afterwards Loch goes to Lugh and asks to be spared and during this conversation he promises safety from the Fomorians thenceforth, grants Lugh infallible judgment, and names Lugh's nine chariots, charioteers, goads, and horses. Following this the Tuatha De capture Bres and he pleads with Lugh to spare his life, eventually offering the secret of farming to the Tuatha De in exchange for his life. After this episode Lugh, the Dagda, and Ogma go to rescue the Dagda's harp and harper from Fomorian custody.

The Lebor Gabala Erenn – The Lebor Gabala Erenn exists in fragments and large sections in various sources and has been dated to roughly the 11th century. This multivolume set of texts contains a great deal of detail about assorted mythic and pseudohistorical figures but not in the story format we usually expect. Much of the text reads more like a list or rough accounting of events. The Tuatha De Danann appear in book IV, following their predecessors the Fir Bolg who they displaced in a story told in depth in the Cét-Cath Maige Tuired. The Lebor Gabala Erenn is also a text which we have multiple variant versions of, not all of which entirely agree with each other. I will try to summarize Lugh's appearance throughout this material here, including the variations found in the different redactions.

Lugh appears early in the Lebor Gabala Erenn, initially mentioned in the opening section describing the four treasures that the Tuatha De brought with them when they arrived in Ireland. The spear is said to belong to Lugh and to be a weapon that no battle could be sustained against. Lugh is mentioned again shortly thereafter in a paragraph about his foster mother Tailtiu. We are told of Lugh's parentage, including that another name for his father Cian mac Dian Cecht was Scál Balb which means 'silent being' or 'silent hero'. This section also details Lugh's founding of the festival of Lunasa in honour of Tailtiu after she exhausts herself clearing plains for crops and dies.

Next, we are told about Lugh's defeat of his grandfather Balor in the battle against the Fomorians (although we learn of this event in much greater detail in the Cat Maige Tuired). The Lebor Gabala Erenn version simply says that in the battle after Nuada's death Lugh took the kingship of the Tuatha De Danann and killed Balor with a sling stone. Lugh then ruled as king of the Tuatha De for 40 years.

We are then given a list of Lugh's paternal ancestry back six generations which are, beginning with his father: Cian, Dian Cecht, Esarg, Net, Indiu, and Alldui; his mother Ethniu is mentioned separately. According to the Lebor Gabala Erenn Lugh: *"is the first who brought chess-play and ball-play and horse-racing and assembling into Ireland"* (Macalister, 1944). The reference to chess play here is to the strategy board game of fidchell, about which little is known. The text also goes on to describe Lugh's kingship after Nuada's death:

"Lugh the spear-slaughterous was made king--
the many-crafted who cooled not.
Forty to Lugh--it was balanced--

in the kingship over the Palace of Banba [i.e. Ireland]"
(Macalister, 1944)

While this passage is short it mentions one of Lugh's epithet's 'rind-agach' which Macalister here gives as spear slaughterous although I favour 'spear combative'. It also mentions that Lugh 'cooled not' a reference I believe to his temper, which is well illustrated in the later tale Oidheadh Chloinne Tuireann.

The next series of passages touch on how various members of the Tuatha De Danann meet their deaths, and we find Lugh mentioned in reference to several people whom he killed. In some versions of the death of Balor Carn Ui Net is specified as the location; here we find that this is the place that Lugh brought about the death of Bres as well. After the Cath Maige Tuired Bres's life had been spared but sometime later Lugh kills him by tricking him into drinking poisonous bog water which Bres believed was milk. The following text also tells us that Lugh brought about the deaths of Brian, Iuchar, and Iucharba, who the Lebor Gabala Erenn calls the three gods of the Tuatha De Danann (elsewhere they are known as the children of Tuireann). By this account Lugh kills them himself, although the later Oidheadh Chloinne Tuireann gives the story in full and offers an alternate explanation of Lugh's involvement. Finally, there is Cermait, son of the Dagda, who Lugh kills after Cermait had an affair with one of Lugh's wives.

The killing of Cermait[6] is a pivotal event and next we learn that Lugh himself was killed by Cermait's son Mac Cuill. A different redaction of the Lebor Gabala Erenn says that it was all three sons of Cermait together who killed Lugh, to avenge their father. This sort of revenge killing mirrors Lugh's own vendetta against the sons of Tuireann for killing his father Cian.

Oidheadh Chloinne Tuireann – This story includes a partial retelling of events in the Cath Maige Tuired, although with a very different perspective[7]. The text itself can only be found in later forms written after the 16th century but as is often the case may be based on earlier material or oral traditions. It casts the Tuatha De Danann in a very different light than they appear in the pre-Norman material and so should be read with an understanding that the later date and cultural influences affect the text.

As this story begins Lugh is in Teamhair where Nuada is king over the Tuatha De Danann when they learn that the Fomorians have attacked the area held by Bodb Derg in Connacht. Lugh urges Nuada to fight but the king refuses, so Lugh leaves angry and encounters his father Cian and uncles Cu and Cethen, here said to be sons of Cainte. He tells his kinsmen the problem and they agree to fight with him and to gather the Riders of the Sidhe to his cause. The three older warriors then set off and split up at which point Cian sees three armed men coming his way. Fearing what they may do he uses a druid's wand to change himself into the shape of a pig and hides among a herd of pigs nearby, but the warriors had already seen him and pursue him anyway. The warriors are the three sons of Tuireann: Brian, Iuchar, and Iucharba. Brian turns his brothers into hounds and they chase down the magical pig until Brian finally throws his spear and impales it. Cian asks to be allowed to change back into his human form, which is granted, and then asks for mercy but Brian refuses saying that he would kill him seven times over. The brothers then stone Cian to death and bury his body. The ground keeps pushing Cian out until the seventh time the brothers bury him. Once they get him to stay buried, they head off to join Lugh's battle with the Fomorians.

Meanwhile Lugh has gone on to confront the Fomorians. Here we find Bres who sees Lugh coming and comments that it is like the sun rising in the west, but the Fomorian druids correct him saying that it is the face of Lugh approaching them. Lugh orders them to return what they have taken from Bodb Derg but, of course, they refuse. Lugh then waits three days until

Bodb Derg's troops and his two uncles Cu and Cethan with the Riders of the Sidhe arrive and then gives battle to the gathered Fomorians, who are routed. Bres and the Fomorians Druids ask for quarter from Lugh and are spared. Lugh then asks his own people where his father is and is told that he did not arrive for the battle, after which Lugh correctly guesses that Cian must have been killed.

Lugh and the riders of the sidhe set off to find out what happened to Cian, and when they arrive at the spot where he was pursued the earth itself offers testimony, telling Lugh about his father's distress and death at the hands of the sons of Tuireann. Following this lead the group uncovers Cian's body and Lugh is heartbroken. He mourns his father with an eloquent speech about the crime that has occurred, then Cian is reburied and a grave cairn raised over him. The group sets off to return to Teamhair but Lugh tells them not to speak of what has happened until he himself reveals it.

Lugh re-joins the assembled Tuatha De Danann at Nuada's court and asks the entire assembly what fine they would ask of men who had killed their father; the group replies with outraged suggestions before asking him if he is talking about the death of his own father Cian to which he replies yes. The sons of Tuireann are very uneasy knowing that he is talking about them but they eventually decide to speak up in front of everyone and admit their guilt, although, when Brian speaks, he doesn't outright admit what they have done, only acknowledges that he knows Lugh suspects them. Having made this acknowledgement and agreed to pay the fine for Cian's death Lugh then sets a list of nearly impossible tasks for them to accomplish in order to bring him back a series of wonderous items. He tricks them into agreeing by initially disguising the exact nature of the items he wants, asking them to get him three apples, the skin of a pig, a spear, two horses, a chariot, seven pigs, a puppy, a cooking-spit, and three shouts on a hill. He tells them if that is too much to refuse and he will ask for less but because it sounds simple, although they are suspicious, they agree. Only then does Lugh reveal which exact items they must recover: the apples are magical apples from a garden in the east of the world, the pig skin is in Greece and will heal anyone it touches and turn water poured through it into wine, the spear is a magical spear from Persia that's head must be kept in water to soothe its burning when not in battle, the horses and chariot belong to a king named Dobar and they can run across water or land equally as fast, the pigs belong to king Easal and can be killed and return to life the next day and no one who eats them will ever get sick, the puppy is named Fail-Inis and belongs to a king of the north and she is beautiful and fierce, the cooking spit belongs to the women of the island of Caer Cennfhinne, and finally the three shouts on the hill must be given on a hill in Lochlann belonging to the people with whom Cian was educated and who allow no one to shout on that place.

The sons of Tuireann go to their father for advice and he tells them to ask Lugh for help, saying that only with the help of Manannán or Lugh could anyone accomplish these feats. He tells them to ask Lugh for the loan of Manannan's horse Aonbharr, because if Lugh really wants the items, he will loan the horse. But if he refuses Tuireann tells them to ask for the loan of Manannan's boat because Lugh has a taboo against refusing two requests. Lugh refuses the horse but loans the boat and the three brothers set off. They have a series of adventures to gain the various items which make up the bulk of the tale.

After acquiring the puppy, Lugh is aware that they may succeed and to prevent this he uses druidic magic on them to make them forget the remaining two items. Believing they have competed their tasks the three brothers head home and go to give Lugh what he has requested. Lugh avoids them but relays through a messenger that the items should be given to the king who in turn gives them to Lugh. Of course, Lugh then asks the brothers in front of the entire assembly about the last two items and they realize that they have come back without fulfilling the entire fine.

The brothers set out again and manage to get the cooking spit but are mortally wounded giving the three shouts on the hill. The manage to get back to their father and ask him to bring the spit and word of the shouts to Lugh and ask him for use of the pig skin which will heal them. Lugh refuses. Tuireann then returns with Brian who is near death and Brian asks for the skin from Lugh but is again refused. Lugh says that he would not let them be healed by it if they could bring him enough gold to cover the world because he wants them to die for the crime they have committed.

After this Brian returns to his brothers and all three die together. Tuireann is so broken hearted over this that he also dies from grief and the four are buried all together.

Tuatha De Danann na Set Siom – Partially prose and partially poem this myth relates how the Tuatha De Danann acquired their 'treasures', four items of special power and renown. Lugh possesses one of these treasures which is usually described as a spear. In the prose section we are told that Lugh possessed the spear and no battle could be sustained against it, while in the poetic section we are told, in contradiction, that it is the sword which belongs to Lugh while the spear is Nuada's.

This myth also relates how the Tuatha De Danann arrived in Ireland, and tells us that Lugh was intentionally left behind so that he could not contest for the kingship with Nuada.

Baile an Scáil – This story takes place during the wider tales of Conn, as part of the Cycle of kings. In this particular episode Conn has just defeated the kings in Ireland and taken his place in Teamhair. Every day he and his druids had the habit of going up to the ramparts of their fort to look out over the land to make sure that the aos sidhe [fairy folk] hadn't taken over Ireland and one day Conn stepped on a particular stone which cried out beneath his foot. His druid wouldn't explain this to him until a set amount of time – 53 days – had passed then revealed that the stone he had stepped on was the Lia Fáil[8].

Immediately after this the group is surrounded by an unearthly mist and hear the sound of an approaching horse. The rider throws three spears at them, the last of which hits the ground first. At that Conn's druid says that whoever is attacking them is attacking the king and the horseman stops, welcoming them and inviting them to follow him to his home. The group follows until they arrive at a plain with a golden tree and a large house with a roof of white-bronze. Inside the building is a gold vat hooped in silver, filled with a red ale, and with a gold dipper on the barrel; there is a young woman in the house wearing a gold crown and holding a gold cup. Sitting on a throne is a royal figure who identifies himself as Lugh sone of Eithne, although he emphasizes that he isn't a phantom (literally scál) and was human and descendant of a pseudo-historical Irish king named Tigernmas. Despite this blending of older folklore and euhemerization Lugh goes on to predict Conn's reign as king and name the kings who will follow him.

The girl is identified as the Sovereignty of Ireland and she serves Conn his meal and then asks Lugh who she shall give a drink from the cup to. After eating and hearing the prophecy of the kings Lugh's shadow covers them all and the house and figures disappeared but Conn was left with the gold and silver vat, gold dipper, and gold cup.

Ulster Cycle – Lugh appears in several places in the heroic epic of the Ulster Cycle which is made up of many smaller sub stories.

Compert Con Culainn – The birth of Cu Chulainn is a complex tale which, properly, features the hero being conceived three times before finally being born as the figure that would feature in the myths. Lugh's role in the story is initially obscure, as he first appears as an unnamed Otherworldly man who has either been keeping king Conchobar's sister Deichtire and her handmaidens for several years in his Otherworldly brugh or is hosting Conchobar and his men, including Deichtire, after they lose their way in the snow.

In a version retold in part by McCone Conchobar, his men and Deichtire (here listed as Conchobar's daughter) are pursuing magical birds when they take shelter in a sidhe. Inside they find a man and pregnant woman who subsequently gives birth to a son; the next morning the man, woman, and sidhe have vanished and Deichtire takes the infant. The baby dies shortly thereafter. Then Deichtire dreams of the man from the sidhe who tells her that he is Lugh and that she is pregnant with his child who is the same baby that died before and will be named Setanta. However, rumours spread that Conchobar is the baby's father so that Deichtire chooses to abort the foetus. She is then married to Sualtam, conceives for the third time and successfully gives birth to Setanta who will later come to be known as Cu Chulainn.

In an alternate version that can be found in the public domain on Mary Jone's Celtic Collective website we are told that Deichtire, in this version Conchobar's sister, disappeared along with 50 handmaidens for the space of three years. Afterwards they returned in the shape of birds to lure the men of Ulster into hunting after them. While on the track of these mysterious birds Conchobar and his retinue encountered a strange home occupied by a man, his wife, and many maidens. Conchobar as the king of Ulster requested the woman's company for the night but she asked that he wait as she was in labour. The next morning the home, man, woman, and handmaidens had disappeared leaving behind only a newborn in Conchobar's cloak; the baby was named Setanta and given to Conchobar's other sister Finncheom to care for. The story ends by revealing that the woman was

Deichtire and the man was Lugh, and their child would come to be known as Cu Chulainn (Jones, 2020).

Táin Bó Cúailnge – Lugh has a small but important part in the Táin Bó Cúailnge where he comes to the aid of his half-human child Cu Chulainn.

In the first recension version of the Táin Bó Cúailnge after fighting against the Morrigan in several animal forms and then against many human warriors Cu Chulainn has been gravely injured. He is with his charioteer Laeg observing the assembled army of Connacht when Laeg spots an Otherworldly figuring passing unseen through the assembly. Cu Chulainn says the man must be a friend of his among the fairy folk but when the man arrives Cu Chulainn doesn't recognize him and asks him who he is to which the man replies: *"I am your father, Lug mac Ethlend, from the fairy mounds."* (O'Rahilly, 1976). Lugh then puts Cu Chulainn into a magical sleep for three days and heals all his wounds, chanting a battle incitement over Cu Chulainn as well. It is strikingly similar to the battle incitements that appear in the Cath Maige Tuired, beginning and ending with the word 'arise', likely indicating that this was a format for such magic. While Cu Chulainn is healing, Lugh takes on his appearance and guards the border in his son's place to keep Connacht from gaining any ground while Cu Chulainn rests.

In alternate versions it is established in the same passage that Cu Chulainn has some familiarity with the people of the sidhe and presumably by extension with his Otherworldly father. In this passage his charioteer Laeg sees a man passing through the army of Connacht as if he were invisible and relays this to Cu Chulainn who declares the man one of the sidhe-folk and one of his fairy-kin.

Dindshenchas – The Dindshenchas are an array of stories describing how certain places came to be named; the collected texts date to around the 11th century. These stories were collected into different groupings including the Metrical Dindshenchas and the Rennes Dindshenchas. Although these short stories do not always agree with other mythology or each other they do present us wonderful titbits of information about Lugh and his associations. References to Lugh here will be organized by the part and section they occur in.

Part III

Cnogba – this tale is about how Cnogba, or Cnoc Bui [hill of Bui], got its name, after Bua Lugh's wife. It refers to Lugh as 'Lug mac Cein of the red spears'

Nás – here we learn that two of Lugh's wives, Bui and Nás, were sisters and that both had places named after them when they died. The section discusses their death and that of Tailtiu and talks about Lugh's institution of memorial games and assembly in their honour.

Carn Hui Neit – this passage is particularly interesting as it relates the tale of how Lugh killed Bres. It does not mention the events of the Cath Maige Tuired or Bres's failed kingship over the Tuatha De Danann but rather speaks of Bres in glowing terms as kind, generous, and full of excellence. Despite this Nechtan,[9] who is the king of Munster at the time, and Lugh join together to bring about Bres's death through trickery and magic. Nechtan orders all the milk cows in his territory to be singed and covered in ash; 300 wooden cows of the same colour are then made and filled with what is described as a red liquid. Lugh uses magic to make them seem like living cows and Bres is challenged to drink a bucket's worth from each one. He is under a prohibition against refusing a challenge of skill and so he accepts and drinks. The liquid, of course, kills him, and he is buried at the site.

Part IV

Tailtiu – Lugh is mentioned briefly here in relation to his founding of the Lughnasadh assembly to honour his foster mother.

Tráig Thuirbe – Another brief mention of Lugh in this passage says that the Fomorians fled before him.

Loch Lugborta – the place name story for Loch Lugborta, lake of Lugh's death, tells of how the children of Cermait had their revenge for the death of their father at Lugh's hands. The three brothers called a meeting with Lugh at Usnech, supposedly to make peace with him after he killed their father because of jealousy over Cermait and Lugh's wife. The truth was the three had formed a plan to kill Lugh and when he arrived Mac Cuill pinned his foot to the ground with a spear. Lugh managed to escape to a nearby lake but there he was drowned. A cairn which was named the Sidan or Carn Lugdach was built over him as his grave and the grave site and lake were both named for him.

Lugh's Arrival at Tara – there is a short portion of a poem which occurs in a larger piece called '"Mór ar bhfearg riot, ri Saxan". This dates to the 14th century and describes Lugh's arrival at Teamhair during the Cath Maige Tuired. It offers details that don't appear in the other version and offers a different perspective on the incident.

Because it is short, I will include my translation of the poem here. The poem offers some good insight into Lugh's personality.

Revealed to Lugh, lover of Teamhra
in the east in Eamhain,
so he went to search the whole earth for
Té's Ramparts, Teamhair [Tara].

closed was the city against Lugh's arrival,
the choicest of warriors;
touched with force the sharp-sided, smooth ramparts
struck the door-wood.

The King's doorman said to the great warrior,
whose anger was swift:
"From where comes the man, keen, young,
bright flower, red cheeked."

To the King's Doorman
said Lugh who never hesitated in reciprocal wounding:
"I am myself a poet of Eamhain Abhlach
of swans and yews."

"Not merited", said Teamhair's doorman,
"Coming from conflict;"

Folklore – Not only does Lugh feature prominently throughout much of the mythology but he can also be found in later folklore where he retained an important role.

There are various folkloric accounts of Lugh and Balor's fight most of which claim Carn Ui Neit was the place at which Balor was killed (Gray, 1983). In these versions the two may still fight during the Cath Maige Tuired but their ultimate confrontation occurs elsewhere.

One of the variant versions of the birth of Lugh is found in folklore particular to Donegal, an account of which can be found in the 1894 book 'Hero-Tales of Ireland' by Curtin. In this account, stripped of implicit divinity, Balor is living on Tory island off the coast of Donegal where he has retreated after hearing a prophecy that he will never die until he is killed by the son of his only daughter. To prevent this, he hides himself and his daughter in a keep surrounded by bells. However, it comes to pass that Balor sends his servants to steal a magical cow, and the smith who the cow is stolen from sends someone to recover it. That man, Fin, gains an ally among the fairies as he seeks the cow and that ally then helps him to meet the challenges Balor lays out to get the cow back. The first is to eat seven cow hides within a short amount of time, which Fin succeeds at because his fairy friend, who is invisible, takes the hides as quickly as Fin can cut them up into pieces. The second challenge is to have Balor's daughter throw the cow's halter to him. To accomplish this the fairy man sneaks Fin into the daughter's room after advising him to persuade her to throw him the halter and then to 'be as intimate with' the other women as he had with Balor's daughter so that they will not speak of his presence there (Curtin, 1894, p 287). Having done this the daughter throws the bridle to him the next day and Fin leaves with the cow.

The following year the fairy man returns to Fin and tells him that they must go to the island and rescue the children he fathered with the women before Balor finds out what has happened and kills them. The pair get away with the children but sailing back across the water 12 of them fall into the ocean and turn into seals; only Balor's grandson is kept safe.

The child wasn't thriving though and on the advice of the fairy man he was brought back to Tory Island. Fin's friend promised Balor to cover the island in trees if he would allow the baby to nurse from the women saying that the child had a magical power to nurse from any woman who held him. Balor was deceived this way for several years until a storm revealed the trees to be enchantment. Fin and his son and fairy friend fled, but eventually Balor's men find Fin and kill him. His son, named Lui Lamvada in the tale, eventually ends up killing two of Balor's men and Balor himself leaves Tory Island to seek revenge. He has a terrible eye in his forehead that burns anything it looks on to ash and he keeps it covered with nine shields. He plans to use this eye to get his revenge but as he is lifting the ninth shield Lui thrusts a red-hot spear into it. Dying Balor tries to trick Lui by telling him to remove Balor's head and hold it over his own to gain all knowledge but instead Lui places the head on a stone pillar; a single drop of liquid from the head creates a great pit in the earth.

In an alternate account, also from Donegal, related by Dáithí O hOgain in his 'Lore of Ireland' we find Balor living on Tory Island with Ethniu to prevent the prophecy from being fulfilled. But in this version when Cian has his tryst with her, he is caught and killed and Ethniu and her infant are put out to sea on a boat. They are found by a smith, Goibhleann [i.e. Goibhniu] who saves them. Later, Balor steals Goibhleann's magical cow and so the smith and Lugh set off to recover it; this counter theft motivates Balor to go on a rampage in Ireland which ends when he arrives at the smith's forge and Lugh puts his eye out with a spear.

This is a loose summary of the highlights of Lugh across Irish mythology. It is in no way definitive and there are other examples where Lugh appears or is referenced, such as the Tochmarc Emire or Dunaire Fionn. For the purposes of this text however I believe these recapping's are enough to give the reader a strong feeling for Lugh's place in Irish myth and his importance, as well as his overall role among the Tuatha De Danann.

End Notes

1   There are interesting parallels between Lugh and the Dagda. They are very different deities in temperament, with the Dagda described as jovial and wise while Lugh is hot-tempered and fierce. Yet among the Tuatha De Danann both are renowned for their multitude of skills; the Dagda earns his name [Dagda, literally good or excellent God] after proclaiming that he will match the promised skills offered by all the others before a battle and two of Lugh's epithets, Ildanach and Samildanach, relate to the multitude of skills he possessed.

2   Death seems at best to be a transitory state for the Tuatha De Danann and one which they recover from easily.

3   The word here is dán which Gray translates as art but which

can mean a variety of things including skill, talent, or even fate.

4   The text specifies that they switch seats for '13 days' although the rest of the story takes place across many years. This may seem like a confusing detail but references to time in the myths are rarely, in my opinion, literally measures but rather symbolic.

5   This incitement is not translated by Gray but I have done a version which can be found in my translation work and Isolde Carmody of Story Archaeology also has done a version. I recommend people interested read both for an idea of the contents. This battle incitement was part of a wider pattern of such in Irish warfare and is very poetic and evocative. It was designed to urge one's own side to win and demoralize the enemy.

The specific pose that Lugh engages in for this incitement is sometimes called the Crane Pose and is practiced as part of a wider type of Irish sorcery called corrguinecht.

6   The death of Cermait and his subsequent resurrection by the Dagda is a fascinating story that appears in a short text often called 'How the Dagda Got His Magic Staff'. It may also illustrate the transient nature of death among the gods, although that lack of actual death doesn't stop the revenge killings we find throughout the stories.

7   The Oidheadh Chloinne Tuireann is a later medieval tale written possibly as much as 6 hundred years after the Cath Maige Tuired was recorded and it has been suggested that the significant alterations in the narrative around Nuada and Lugh reflect the politics of the 16th century in Ireland.

8   The Lia Fáil – literally stone of the enclosure, figuratively stone of Ireland – is one of the four treasures of the Tuatha De Danann, and the only such treasure that had no explicitly named owner. The Lia Fáil would cry out under the touch of the rightful king and was seen as both a symbol of sovereignty and representing the will of the sovereign

goddess(es) of Ireland. According to several sources in myth including the Lebor Gabala Erenn the stone was silenced by Cu Chulainn who struck it when it failed to cry out under his foster sun Lugaid.

9   Nechtan is possibly an alternate name for Nuada, who is in various sources called Nuada Necht and who several scholars suggest may be identical to both Nechtan and Elcmar. If this is so, in this particular tale, it would provide the motivation for Nechtan/Nuada and Lugh to conspire against Bres.

Chapter 3

Lleu, Lugus, and Fionn

"...said [Arianrhod] 'the fair one strikes it with a skilful hand!'
'Aye,' [Gwydion] replied '.... He has obtained a name, and the name
is good enough "Lleu Skillful Hand" he will be from now on.'"
Parker, 2003

Lugh was a pan-Celtic deity who can be found under similar names in different related cultures, although one should note the mythology is very different elsewhere. Scholars generally agree that the Irish Lugh, Welsh Lleu, and Gaulish Lugos are connected deities although how closely they may be linked is debated. This overlapping of name and symbolism can sometimes create confusion between the various cognates of Lugh and there are instances where the mythology or symbols of one are attributed to another by people who are treating the three as one conjoined topic. An example of this can be found in the writing of Marie-Louise Sjoestedt, renowned in her time for her Celtic studies focus, who gives Lugudunum [modern Lyon in France] as 'fortress of Lugh' rather than the more accurate fortress of Lugus, blurring the lines completely between the Irish and Gaulish deities.

There has also been some supposition connecting Lugh to the mythic hero of Fionn mac Cumhall. There are arguments on both sides of this debate which we will discuss in depth in this chapter, however just like relating Lugh to Lugus or Lleu the debate can be boiled down to whether or not a person sees Lugh as unique from Fionn or sees Fionn as an aspect or variant version of Lugh.

Whether or not these all represent Lugh through different cultural interpretations or are different deities who may all share a common root in the same original deity is a question that can never be entirely answered. There are people who see all three as the same deity interpreted through various cultural lenses but there are also those who strongly feel that while the three may share a common source, they are different and unique deities. I encourage readers to make up their own minds as to which theory they believe but to also consider each deities' mythology on its own merits.

Lleu Llaw Gyffes

The Welsh cognate to the Irish Lugh is found in the mythic material known as the Mabinogion under the name Lleu Llaw Gyffes[1] which means (like the Irish) Lleu of the long arm. The myths of the two figures show some striking similarities but also some profound differences. To illustrate this, I would like to briefly recap Lleu's mythology.

We find Lleu's stories most prominently in the 4th branch of the Mabinogi. Lleu's mother was Arianrhod but his birth story is an unusual tale which begins with the story of his mother being tested in the court as a foot holder for her uncle Math. Math required a virgin's lap to rest his feet in when he wasn't at war and was seeking a replacement. His nephew Gwydion suggested Math's niece Arianrhod (Gwydion's sister) but when she stepped over the magic wand that Math used to test her claim to be a maiden, she immediately birthed a son; this was Dylan who would have a great affinity for the sea. When the child was born Arianrhod fled the room in shame and as she fled another small thing fell from her which Gwydion[2] scooped up and put in a chest near his bed; this was the child that would be Lleu. One day sometime later Gwydion heard a baby crying and opening up the chest he found an infant which he took to a woman to be nursed. The baby grew twice as quickly as any other child and at two years old was the size of a child of four and came to live with Gwydion. The two eventually went to visit

Arianrhod but she was outraged when she learns the identity of the boy. She swore that he would never have a name unless she gives him one, so Gwydion set out to trick her into it, getting her to admire a clever stone cast by the boy, while the two were in disguise as show makers. When she remarks of the boy that he is 'the fair one [who] has a clever hand' Gwydion immediately declared that to be his name – Lleu Llaw Gyffes. Angered again Arianrhod said that the boy would never be given weapons unless she herself gave them so Gwydion once again set out to trick her into doing so. This time he disguised himself and Lleu to get into Arianrhod's castle before making her think they were under attack; trying to defend her place she arms the two. Upon finding out about this second trick she said that Lleu would never get a wife of any people then on earth.

Just as his birth story and childhood are unusual so is the way in which he acquires a wife and the events that occur because of that. Since his mother had declared he would never find a wife on earth his uncle Gwydion and his great uncle Math created a maiden for him out of three types of flowers: oak, broom, and meadowsweet. This maiden was named Blodeuedd and she became Lleu's wife. However, she was not happy with this arrangement and she took a lover Gronw Pebyr who was lord of an adjoining land. The two decided to kill Lleu so that they could be together and to do so Blodeuedd tricked Lleu into revealing the only circumstances under which he could be killed, which involved a convoluted set of circumstances. To make such circumstances happen Blodeuedd further convinced Lleu to demonstrate for her, thus giving her lover the opportunity to try to kill him. Gronw Pebyr cast a poisoned spear at Lleu which pierced his body, but Lleu transformed into an eagle and fled. Gwydion was distraught and began to search the world (or at least Wales) for Lleu. Eventually Gwydion found Lleu, still shaped as an eagle, perched high in an oak tree between two lakes. He was perpetually dying but not dead. Gwydion chanted a poem to him and the eagle moves down a bit, and another poem is chanted and the eagle gets closer and finally a third poem and the eagle falls into Gwydion's arms. Gwydion used a magic wand to give Lleu back his proper shape but it took a year for him to return to health.

When he had regained his health Lleu went to Math to seek justice against Gronw Pebyr and Blodeuedd; Math agreed that he had a right to such. Gwydion pursued Blodeuedd as she tried to flee and upon capturing her transformed her into an owl and gave her the name of Blodeuwedd[3]. Lleu in turn went after Gronw Pebyr, who sent an envoy to him trying to parlay but Lleu said he would be satisfied with nothing less than Gronw Pebyr taking the same spear blow from Lleu that he had cast at him. Gronw had no choice but to accept, although he asked that he be allowed to hold a stone up as a shield since he had acted on the advice of another; Lleu allowed this but cast his spear through the stone anyway killing Gronw Pebyr. And it was said after that Lleu was lord over his land for many years.

MacKillop associates Lleu with oaks and eagles and suggests that his appearance in the Mabinogion reflects what was likely a much greater importance in Welsh mythology, later obscured by Christian redactors. Many authors in discussing Lleu compare him directly to Lugh and frame his mythology in the context of Lugh's stories, creating some confusion particularly in modern pagan material between the two.

Lugus

Lugus, or Lugos, is the Gaulish version of Lugh and arguably the oldest of the three deities who share versions of this name. The main theory for the meaning of Lugus, as with Lugh, connects it to proto-Indo-European roots including 'oath', however the later Gaulish would attach the meaning of bird or raven to it (MacKillop, 1998). There are hints that birds may have been associated with Lugus or formed part of his imagery (Sjoestedt,

2000). Nonetheless the connection to the root word for oath, in Gaulish lugio, lends itself to the interpretation of Lugus as a god of oaths like Lugh (O hOgain, 2006).

As with many Gaulish deities very little is directly known about him and most of what we do know comes from inscriptions that have been found. These inscriptions can be difficult to interpret but several are objects dedicated in Lugus's name and his divinity is generally not questioned. His wider importance is assumed based on the use of his name in place names, such as the city of Lugudunum in France, now known as Lyon. These place names connected to Lugh can be found across what was Gaul and in what are now England and Scotland (MacKillop, 1998). Inscriptions to him are focused mostly in the Iberian Peninsula.

Lugus is thought in some cases to be a triple deity, that is a grouping of three identically named deities or similar gods. This pattern of triples is very common across Celtic cultures, although it must be noted that it is radically different from the modern neopagan triple deity concept. The historic view of triple deities usually had them as siblings or age-equals, sometimes literal triplets. There are theories that Lugus may be such a triple deity, based in part on images thought to be Lugus that depict three heads or three men standing together and in part by variations of Lugh's birth story that say he had two brothers born with him who escaped into the sea and became seals. Combining the cross-cultural mythology with the imagery has caused some scholars to suspect such a triple nature for Lugus.

The Romans tended to look at the gods of other cultures through the Interpretatio Romana, a lens that saw the gods of other cultures as Roman gods under different names. Because of this when talking about foreign deities, Roman writers usually called them by Roman names, making it difficult to identify exactly which deity was being referred to in the native culture. This means that scholars must resort to context clues and guesses to try to match known deities to their recorded counterparts.

Lugus is strongly connected by scholars to the 'Gaulish Mercury' mentioned by Julius Caesar, so much so that it is nearly taken for granted that this connection is certain. MacKillop suggests two main reasons for this: Caesar calls the Gaulish Mercury the creator of all arts which is very similar to Lugh's epithet of master of all arts, and a connection between Lugus and Mercury in several place names. This Gaulish Mercury was, according to Caesar, the most popular of the Gaulish deities and he wrote:

"They worship as their divinity, Mercury in particular, and have many images of him, and regard him as the inventor of all arts, they consider him the guide of their journeys and marches, and believe him to have great influence over the acquisition of gain and mercantile transactions"
(McDevitte & Bohn, 2012).

Like his Irish counterpart Lugus had a harvest celebration around the beginning of August. This festival was co-opted and repurposed by the Romans into an event for the emperor Augustus (O hOgain, 2006). This harvest festival along with the other hints we have about Lugus's purviews reinforce his connection to the Welsh Lleu and Irish Lugh. O hOgain suggests that Lugus was likely the template for the later insular versions of the deity, suggesting that his worship spread to Wales and Ireland around the beginning of the common era.

Fionn Mac Cumhall

Irish mythology is often divided into various cycles, such as the mythic cycle, Ulster cycle, and cycle of kings. Another cycle of stories are those of Fionn and the Fianna, called the Fenian cycle. The stories centre on Fionn mac Cumhall and his close relatives including Oisín and Caelte.

Fionn is a semi-historical figure in Irish mythology, sometimes viewed as pseudohistorical and other times as divine. His father

45

Cumhall was a warrior who was killed before he was born and because of the danger to his life from his father's enemies he was put into fosterage with several women, renowned as Druids and warriors. Fionn gained great knowledge when he put his thumb in his mouth, after having scalded it on a potion meant to convey wisdom to whoever consumed it. He was known as a great warrior, poet, and leader of the Fianna. There are various locations in Ireland associated with him and he survived into modern folklore in several places. His stories also associate him with Telltown and the tale of Fionn's shield says that it was made from some of the hazel tree in which Lugh placed Balor's head.

For many people Fionn is his own personage and possibly deity but some people see Fionn as potentially an avatar or later form of the god Lugh, something that Williams discusses at length in his book 'Ireland's Immortals'. MacKillop also suggests this connection, stating that both Fionn and Cu Chulainn may be incarnations of Lugh and pointing out that Fionn's name means 'light' or 'white' which is one potential interpretation of Lugh's name. There are accounts of the names being combined as 'Fionnlugh' in genealogies which feels may reflect older lore of Fionn and Lugh being synthesized (MacNeill, 1962).

Fionn was the leader of a warband, the Fianna, who were renowned warriors that lived on the fringe of Irish society. The evidence for Fionn having originally been a deity is persuasive and he has a Welsh cognate in Gwynn ap Nudd whose name also means light or white and who leads Otherworldly hunters. Unlike the other Irish deities however Fionn wasn't recorded in the literary record as one of the Tuatha De Danann but later, through an entirely Christian lens, as a human hero. This may have been a sign of the poor regard that the monks had for Fionn's nature and the war bands who were dedicated to him (Williams, 2016). It may also be possible that Fionn and Lugh did begin as one figure and were divided into two based on what aspects the people doing the writing favoured.

Another piece of evidence connecting Lugh to Fionn is that Fionn also may have had a festival held for him around 1 August. Known as Lúnasa now its, probably older, name is Brón Trogain. In one poetic account Fionn claims that there was a feast for him yearly on Brón Trogain (MacNeill, 1962). At the least we can say that both Lugh and Fionn were associated with a harvest festival at the beginning of August, although Lugh's Lúnasa has eclipsed the older festival associated with Fionn. Beyond that it is up to the reader to decide how persuasive they find the evidence connecting these two figures.

End Notes

1   Roughly pronounced Hlew Hlaw Gif-fes.

2   No father is ever named for Lleu but there is much speculation that it may have been Gwydion. Prior to Arianrhod giving birth to the two boys there was another incident where her brother Gwydion and her other brother Gilfaethwy conspired to rape Math's previous foot holder and as a punishment for this Math had the two brothers spend three years in the shape of various paired animals; each year they produced a child which Math would turn from animal form into human and name. Although this was done as a punishment for their crime it does perhaps establish a pattern in the story of incest. Parker also argues in his notes on 'The Mabinogi of Math' that the wordplay which occurs in the Welsh text also hints at this, with the word for boy and son being identical.

3   This is something of a play on words in Welsh. Her original name, Blodeuedd means 'flowers' in Welsh while her new name Blodeuwedd means 'flower face'. I have seen some speculation that she was turned into a barn owl specifically and that the name of flower face is a reference to the distinctive face of those owls. That is purely supposition however.

Chapter 4

Possessions and Associations

"From Gorias was brought the spear which Lugh had. No battle was ever sustained against it, or against the man who held it in his hand" Cath Maige Tuired, Grey translation

I firmly believe that to better understand any deity we need to understand the things that are associated with them. Often these things – items, animals, holy days – will give us insight into the nature and personality of the deities as well as providing a fuller picture of how the deity was understood or viewed in the past. When it comes to Lugh, I believe this is especially true because the modern view of him can be shallow and focus only on very specific connections that he has; looking at the wider view and the breadth of the historic material provides richness and texture to Lugh that is necessary to grasp who he truly is beyond the surface.

Kingship – Kingship is one of the strongest associations we have with Lugh, although he was only one of the succession of kings of the Tuatha De Danann. This may be because he is the king or takes the kingship during the battle with the Fomorians, in one of the most pivotal stories of the corpus. Kim McCone in his 'Pagan Past and Christian Present in Early Irish Literature' describes Lugh as an ideal king and compares him to the Biblical King David, suggesting that the Christian scribes recording the stories would have seen this resemblance and played on it in their own conceptualization of the Irish tales. Williams similarly says that Lugh in literature may have represented *"the potent native dimension of ideal kingship"* and also compares him to King David, who would have represented the ultimate Christian depiction of kingship (Williams, 2016, p23).

Lugh may be seen as one of the kings of the Otherworld, particularly associated with Teamhair, as he is depicted as such in the story of Baile an Scáil (Smyth, 1988). He is also strongly associated with the founding of different mortal family lines and several different tribes were named after him (Smyth, 1988). Lugh was the king of the Gods for a time and is portrayed as having a very important role among the others, being both well-known and appearing in a variety of myths. Some scholars suggest that Lugh was an interloper to the Irish pantheon who was only added later and that his mythology reflects this, showing him being born and coming into the crisis between the Tuatha De Danann and Fomorians in a way that displaces the existing king Nuada (O hOgain, 2006).

The incident that occurs in the story of the Baile an Scáil may also be read as Lugh holding sway over or influencing sovereignty. While this is usually the realm of sovereignty goddesses, and indeed we see such in the story, Lugh also acts as a mediator of kingship here by bringing Conn to the Otherworldly house and directing the sovereignty goddess to give the cup to Conn. Further to this MacKillop mentions Lugh as the consort of Sovereignty in various oral folklore.

Oaths – John Koch in his 1992 paper *'Further to tongu do dia toinges mo thuath'* argues very persuasively for Lugh, and more vitally his older cognates, as a god of oath taking based on both etymology and his origins. There is ample evidence that Lugh's name is connected to the words for oath taking in older Welsh and Irish, llw and luiges respectively, and that the patterned or ritual manner of speaking an oath was based on avoiding directly invoking Lugh's name while obliquely referencing it (Koch, 1992). This pattern of swearing can be found across myth and folklore and utilizes some form of the phrase 'I swear by the God my people swear by' or 'I swear as my people swear'. Although we do not see direct references in the Irish or Welsh material to Lugh being invoked in oaths Koch cites a possible Gaulish example and also says:

> *"it follows that whenever pagan Celts were swearing Lugus was not far off-stage, even when his name was carefully obscured, in fact, especially so when this was done. In the specific texts under consideration the god is still very much resident in our texts."* (Koch, 1992, page 254).

The idea that the god's name would not be directly referenced is based on cultural taboos that would have avoided directly naming such a powerful being. The exact reason for this taboo is uncertain but may be based on the perceived holiness of the being. It is also possible that not directly naming the deity in question might have been done to avoid those outside your own tribal group knowing the name of the deity and then having the ability to petition that deity themselves against you (Koch, 1992). And indeed, the word for oath in older Irish, luige, does have several grammatical forms that are identical to Lugh's name reinforcing both the connection between the two and the need to use a different term to avoid invoking Lugh's name.

Sorcery – When Lugh first enters Teamhair and joins the Tuatha De Danann as they plan to rebel against the Fomorians, he gives a list of his own skills and included in that is sorcery, or in the older Irish coirrguinecht. This term can be broken down to corr = crane and guinech = wound-dealing giving us 'wound-dealing crane' or 'crane-wounding'. The crane aspect likely comes in with the pose that is typically associated with this form of magic; standing on one leg, with one arm behind the back, and one eye closed. We see an example of Lugh using this magic apparently to good effect in the Cath Maige Tuired.

Corrguinecht is associated with what we might call cursing, the term later showing up in reference to stealing milk from a neighbour's cows. Gray discusses Lugh's use of this practice in her notes in the Cath Maige Tuired, connecting corrguinecht to glam dicen, a type of spoken satire that brought a negative effect on those it was cast on. Although we may find this to be a conflict of modern morals for some people historically cursing was seen as a powerful tool for righting injustices and in Irish practice it was believed that to misuse cursing would cause a physical blemish on the caster.

We also see at least one example of Lugh using Druidic magic. This occurs in the Oidheadh Chloinne Tuireann when he sets a spell of forgetfulness on the sons of Tuireann.

Healing – Although rarely focused on now, Lugh does have healing associations. He claims he is a physician when entering Teamhair in the Caith Maige Tuired and he heals Cu Chulainn with herbs and charms in the Táin Bó Cuiliagne. This skill makes sense for the grandson of a healing god and nephew of four other physician deities.

Storms and lightning – Lugh has a strong folk association with storms and lightning and also a tentative one based on his epithets and associations. A proverbial saying in Ballycroy identifies Lugh as a god of storms (MacNeill, 1962). This saying links Balor to him as his father not grandfather: *"The wind of Lugh long-arm is flying in the air tonight. Yes, and the sparks of his father. Balor Béimeann is the father"* (Kondratiev, 1997). Kondratiev saw this as evidence connecting Lugh to storms and suggested that his relation to light was actually to lightning. The word lonn, which appears in several of Lugh's epithets, means fierce, strong, eager, or angry but is an adjective often applied to lightning and found in various phrases about lightning.

The Sun – It is very common in modern books and communities to see Lugh equated to the sun or described as a sun God. There's no direct evidence of this in the source material, although his countenance is described as like the sun, something that we see applied to several of the Tuatha De Danann possibly in relation to their beauty. An example of this for Lugh comes from the Oidheach Chloinne Tuireann:

> *"It is then Bres, son of Elathan, rose up and said: "It is a wonder to me the sun to be rising in the west to-day, and it rising in the east every other day."*
>
> *"It would be better for us it to be the sun," said the Druids.*
> *"What else is it?" said he.*
> *"It is the shining of the face of Lugh, son of Ethlinn," said they."*
> (Cross & Slover, 1936).

Sjoestedt also touches on the misidentification of Lugh as a solar deity, saying:

> *"[Lugh] is called Lámh-fhada ('Lug of the Long Arm') and the epithet refers not to his solar nature as has been supposed, although there is nothing in mythology to confirm it, but to his manner of warfare. Lug can wound from a distance by means of his casting weapons..."* (Sjoestedt. 2000, p 43)

Williams in his book 'Ireland's Immortals' discusses Lugh's late 19th century and early 20th century shift into a sun god in greater detail, pointing out the dearth of source material supporting the idea and noting the later works by writers such as Yeats who depicted him solidly in the solar deity camp likely influenced his popular image. These works seem to have drawn on the Oidheadh Chloinne Tuireann for their inspiration, despite the later date of that material and common usage of 'sun faced' to describe particularly attractive deities (Williams, 2016). MacNeill agrees with this as a source for the later idea of Lugh as a sun god, and O'Rahilly similarly finds later references to Lugh as sun-faced to have led to his association as a solar deity, but sees the sun god as Lugh's opponent in myths rather than Lugh as the sun's embodiment. This later material was undoubtedly heavily influenced by a classical view of deities and the prevailing Romanticism of pagan material prevalent at the time; these factors caused a confirmation bias wherein a person sought evidence of a solar god because they believed there must be one to be found and then fit a likely deity into the pre-made mould. When the wider Irish material is studied, if anything, we find not sun gods but sun goddesses, such as Grian whose name literally means 'sun'.

However, while the idea may be a newer one, born during the Victorian period, it has taken root within both some corners of the academic world and widely within the pagan community. In this school of thought Lugh is equated to the classical Apollo as both an embodiment of the sun and having control over all things solar. Archaeologist John Waddell views Lugh as a *"personification of the sun"* and ties him to the power of the sun at various seasonal times including midwinter (Waddell, 2014, p 33). It is common now for various pagans celebrating Lúnasa or honouring Lugh to emphasize his solar connection and some modern pagan songs to him explicitly connect him to the sun. This view relates his spear or 'long arm' to the rays of the sun and sees him as the beneficial sun in contrast to Balor as the destructive sun.

Spear - Lugh possessed one of the four treasures of the Tuatha De Danann, said in myth to be either a sword or spear, although it is most often believed to be a spear (Daimler, 2015). It is said that whoever had the spear of Lugh could never lose in battle. In the story 'Tuatha De Danand na Set Soim' we are told that this treasure was acquired by Lugh in a city before the Gods came to Ireland, a version echoed in less detail in the Lebor Gabala Erenn, although there is another story about how he gained the spear as well. The Oidheadh Chloinne Tuireann tells us that after Lugh's father Cian was killed by the children of Tuireann, Lugh required them to fulfil a series of impossible tasks and in so doing gained his famous spear.

The kind of spear that Lugh possessed might better be called a javelin in modern English as it is not the heavy spear we might picture but a smaller, lighter spear that was thrown (Sjoestedt, 2000).

Sling – One of Lugh's other well-known weapons was the sling, and he gained the name Lamhfada [long arm] because of it. He used this weapon to good effect in the Cath Maige Tuired by casting a stone which put out the eye of his grandfather Balor.

The sling is a weapon that we see referenced throughout Irish mythology and which was often used to kill important figures; in the Ulster cycle the hero Fergus is killed by a sling cast and the epic queen Medb dies when her nephew, seeking revenge for his mother's death, uses his sling to cast a hardened piece of cheese at her head.

Hound – Lugh is said to have a hound or lap-dog named Failinis (MacKillop, 1998). This name may be a play on words for the name of Ireland itself – Fáil Inis, island of Fáil, where Fáil is an old idiom for Ireland. This dog was acquired for Lugh by the sons of Tuirenn as part of their fine for killing Lugh's father.

Horses, Chariots, and Charioteers – In the Cath Maige Tuired we are told that Lugh possesses nine chariots with names, eight charioteers for them, eight goads, and eleven horses. Here I am going to include the names of all of these items/people/animals as well as suggestions for their possible meanings. Some of the words are obscure or hard to translate but I feel that it can offer insight into Lugh to understand the names of these things associated with him.

The horses are:

Cana - a cub or a poet of the fourth degree
Doriadha - may mean difficult to ride
Romuir - the sea or ocean
Laisad - burning, blazing
Fer Forsaid - old man/wise man
Sroban - Sruban means little loaf or cake
Airchedal - a poem/poetry
Ruagar – obscure but possibly 'red fear' or 'very frightening'
Ilan - much fullness
Allriadha – possibly from oll riata - fully domesticated
Rocedal - great singing/song
The chariots are:
Luachta – possibly 'hard heeled'
Anagat – possibly 'protector' as a variant form of anagal
Achad - pasture
Feochair – fierce or wild
Fer - man
Golla – foreigner (literally Gaulish person)
Fosad - steadfast
Cráeb – branch (or tree)
Carpat – chariot
The charioteers are:
Medol - metal
Medón – middle
Moth – man (literally male being/genitals)
Mothach – prolific
Foimtinne – fire-receiving, although Gray suggests 'readiness'
Tenda – severe or vigorous
Tress – battle
Morb – dead (assuming from marb)
The goads they carried were named:
Fes - knowledge

Res – dream or vision
Roches – possibly 'great spear'
Anagar - protects
Ilach – victory cry
Canna – moth or vessel
Ríadha - domesticated
Búaid - victory

Miscellaneous Items – The Metrical Dindshenchas mention a 'shirt of Lugh' that was made of refined gold. This may be the shirt that some believe gave him his epithet 'leathsuanaigh'.

In the Acallam na Senorach there is a reference to Lugh possessing a magical net, or possibly chain, which can capture 800 warriors at once (Williams, 2016).

Lugh has many possessions of his own but he is also said to have several loaned to him by Manannan who is his foster father. This includes a horse named Aonbharr who can run over water and land and a boat that moves swifter than the wind.

We are told that Lugh has a cloak from the daughters of Flidais although we don't know anything else about this (Cross & Slover, 1936).

Cró Loga – Literally 'Lugh's enclosure' this is a move in a game called fidchell* which Lugh created in the Cath Maige Tuired. What it was exactly is lost to time but in the story, it is used in reference to Lugh winning all the games. Some accounts credit Lugh with the creation of the game of fidchell (Gray, 1983).

Locations – Lugh has a number of places that are explicitly associated with him in mythology and folklore. Some of these, like his fairy hill at Sidhe Rordubán[1], have no clear earthly locations that we know of while others are earthly locations named for him.

Lough – both the county and the town are named after the god Lugh; Lough's Irish name is Lú, the modern Irish spelling of the god's name.

Suidhe Lughaidh, - 'Lugh's Seat' is a cairn located near Loch Arbhach [Lough Arrow] in county Sligo. This site is near a place named for the battle of Maigh Tuired on a hill called Farmaoil na bhFian [round top of the Fianna]. Folklore maintained that mythic beings or giants of old met at this location (Copeland Borelase, 1897).

Dún Lúiche – 'Lugh's Fort' in Donegal.

Rath Lugaide – 'Lugh's Fort' in Carney, co Sligo.

Cnoc Lughdach – Is recorded as an older name for the hill of Tailtiu (MacNeill, 1962). This may be a reflection of the strong association between Lugh and the celebration of Lúnasa at this site or it may reflect even older traditions that connect Lugh to that place.

Rath Lugh – 'Lugh's Fort'. Rath Lugh is a ring fort located in the Gabhra valley in co Meath.

Loch Lugborta – The lake mentioned in the Dindshenchas as the site of Lugh's death and grave is near Uisneach in county West Meath. Uisneach is site of significant cosmological and ritual significance, often viewed as the centre of Ireland and its spiritual heart (McGinley, et al., 2015) On the eastern slope of the hill of Uisneach is Lough Lugh, called Loch Lugborta in the older sources; slightly to the north of the lake is Carn Lughdech. The lake itself was artificially created out of a small marshy area, possibly to have a lake on site for ritual purposes (McGinley, et al, 2015).

Carn Lughdech – Positioned close to Lough Lugh this cairn is alleged to be the grave site of Lugh in the Dindshenchas material. The cairn itself is a bronze age monument that occurs as part of a wider complex of sites connected to Uisenach and includes a created enclosure that hints at ritual activity at the site (McGinley, et al, 2015).

Sid in Broga – Now known as Newgrange. By some accounts this is where Lugh was buried (MacNeill, 1962).

Lúnasa

"Lughnasa that is the assembly of Lugh son of Ethliu that is an assembly [oenach] held by him at the start of the harvest every year at the coming of Lughnasad. Games or assemblies are named nasad" Sanas Cormaic

Lugh is most strongly associated with the festival of Lúnasa, which bears his name, although it is more properly understood as a memorial for his foster mother Tailtiu, or possibly for two of his wives, Buí and Nás. Lúnasa in old Irish is Lugnasad meaning 'funeral assembly of Lugh' while in more modern Irish the name means 'games or assembly of Lugh'. According to the Lebor Gabala Erenn Lugh instituted the games of Lúnasa in honour of his foster mother after she died clearing the plain that bore her name (Macalister, 1941). In the Metrical Dindshenchas we are told that Tailtiu cleared a great forest named Caill Chuan [roughly 'forest of the stick bundles'] so that it became the plain of Bregmag [plain of the hill]. This area is roughly around co Meath and Dublin. The effort was so great that she died[2] and as she lay dying, she asked that memorial games be held in her memory.

The date of the festival's celebration marks the time that she died *"about the calends of August she died, on a Monday"* (Gwyn, 1924). The Dindshenchas accounts of Buí and Nás suggest that the harvest fairs celebrated around the beginning of August were established by Lugh in honour of his two wives after they died. There is likely a deeper symbolic meaning to everything about the Lúnasa fairs, and the commemoration of such events at sites associated with female figures. As Hicks explains it in his article 'The Lughnasa Triangle': *"In the tales, the female characters associated with the oenach sites are said to have been carried off and usually to have died of shame, grief, or other woe as a result. This death seems to symbolize the harvest of the grain."* Hicks, 2012, p 115).

Sites connected to Tailtiu and Nás – Telltown and Naas respectively – have a long-established traditions of these fairs. The main site of the major oenach, or festival, was at Telltown (historically named Tailtiu for the goddess) and this place was not only hugely significant for the Lúnasa assembly but was the seat of power of the Ui Neill's (Williams, 2016). Other locations connected to the harvest fairs sometimes had their own mythology linked only to a female power, such as Carman, although Lugh still tended to feature into the stories in some way. There is also a reference in the Tochmarc Emire to Lugh having his coronation – literally 'wedding feast of kingship' – at Telltown, which may add another layer to the celebrations and games.

The older harvest fairs focused particularly on trading, games of skill, and political meetings. The modern holiday focuses on the celebration of the beginning of the harvest with things like dressing holy wells, horse races, athletic games, and the preparations of special foods. The general air of the celebrations are joyful and to some extent reflect the spirit of the assembly that Tailtiu herself wished for in her final request, asking for a fair that was devoid of dangers and deceit but full of games, music, and feats of body and mind (Gwyn, 1924). Historically the importance of the Lúnasa assemblies cannot be overemphasized and they acted not only as times for trade and games but also for political meetings, judgements of law, and religious occasions for both pagans and later Christians.

Today many Lúnasa celebrations centre on Saint Patrick as a divine protector of the harvest but it is likely that Lugh originally held this role and was only later replaced when the new religion came in (McNeil, 1962). We may perhaps extrapolate from that suggestion that the places where we see saint Patrick featured now, such as fighting against Crom Dubh or Crom Cruach[3] for control of the harvest, would originally have portrayed such a battle between Lugh and Crom. This may be further supported by the way that we see Lugh and Bres interacting after the battle of Maige Tuired, where Bres asks for his life to be spared and Lugh wants something in exchange; Bres makes three offers all relating to agriculture but the first two are refused as unnatural. The third is accepted when Bres offers knowledge of ploughing, planting, and harvesting. MacNeill suggests that this represents Lugh forcefully gaining important knowledge about agricultural success from an antagonistic deity. This may echo similar stories of Lúnasa where saint Patrick – as Lugh's surrogate – gains the harvest from Crom.

Lughnasa is also called Brón Trogain in Irish and in various other Celtic cultures Lunsadal, Laa Luanys, Calan Awst, and Gouel an Eost, and Alexei Kondratiev conjectures that the Celts of Gaul may have called this celebration Aedrinia (Kondratiev, 1998). The many names of the holiday show it's pan-Celtic character, and demonstrate that it could be found across the Celtic world. Several of the names for the holiday are references to the beginning of autumn or of the harvest, such as Brón Trogain which may be read as 'sorrow of the earth'. MacNeill connects a date on the Coligny calendar representing a harvest festival that lines up with the Irish celebration and month of August.

The most well-known Irish name of the festival, Lughnasadh or Lughnasa, can be broken down into Lugh Nasadh and translated into either Middle or Old Irish as the assembly of Lugh or the funeral assembly of Lugh. The connection to a funeral assembly undoubtedly references the belief that the celebration was originally created by the god Lugh as a memorial for his foster mother, Tailtiu, after her death, and the assembly of Lugh is thought to refer to the many athletic games and competitions associated with the harvest fairs that occurred at this time.

The older texts reference Lúnasa being celebrated for two weeks on either side of the 1st of August. Evidence suggests that the actual celebration could vary between 25 July and 12 August, prompting one anthropologist to suggest that the timing of the event was based on a combined luni-solar system (Hicks, 2012). The Lúnasa fairs would last for between one and two weeks during which local communities would gather together to partake in the sports, trading, and meetings that marked the season.

Endnotes

1. This location is named in the Gabail an t-Sida among a list of other fairy hills belonging to various members of the Tuatha De Danann.

2. It is highly likely that this incident had cosmogenical significance and it may reflect an older, now lost, creation story in which a goddess labours to shift entropy into civilization and sacrifices herself in the process.

3   This is further complicated however because Crom Dubh or Crom Cruach may himself by a later literary invention styled after the Christian Devil or antichrist. Despite this, it remains likely that the wider motif of a heroic figure fighting against a figure of entropy to preserve or win the harvest is older and genuine. We may see reflections of this motif in the story of Lugh killing Balor as well Lugh gaining agricultural knowledge from Bres.

Chapter 5

Lugh in the Modern World

"Lugh answered: "I remember the hills and the woods and the rivers of Ireland, and though all my kinsfolk were gone from it and the sea covered everything but the tops of the mountains, I would go back."" Ella Young, 'The Coming of Lugh'

Lugh's importance has changed over time, of course, as Christianity came in, but he has not been relegated to obscurity by any means as some of the other Tuatha De Danann were. Time has shaped people's understandings of Lugh in new direction however which can be shown by looking at his depictions over the last hundred years or so. In this chapter we will look at the way that Lugh has been portrayed in modern retellings of his stories, which often vary significantly from the older mythology, how he has been shown in mass media, and Lugh in modern paganism.

Modern Folklore

We have examined Lugh's place in the older mythology and in older folklore but he can also be found in more recent folklore, some of which has been created by the fertile imaginations of authors during and since the Victorian period. It's important to understand these newer threads and how they have been woven into the older in the last 150 years. It is up to the reader to decide their place and value, but whether you accept or reject them they do form part of our understanding of who Lugh is.

Jeremiah Curtin, Hero-tales of Ireland, 1894 – Lugh continues to be found in modern Irish folklore and as was true historically this folklore can often be very regionally specific. One example of this is seen in Curtin's late 19th century work which preserved folklore from the area of Donegal and gives us versions of the Lugh and Balor story that are largely different from older mythology. Curtin's retelling has been presented already in chapter 2 so it won't be recapped again however one key change to be emphasized here is the shifting of Lugh (called Lui in the story) into a wholly human figure. This sort of euhemerization is common in later material and Williams in 'Ireland's Immortals' notes the prevalence of historic and ancestral figures named Lugh or with names that are variants of Lugh who are described in fully human terms yet are certainly meant to be reflections of the older deity.

W. B. Yeats – also writing in the late 1890's we find Yeats, a poet and amateur folklorist, as well as occultist. Yeats wrote of Lugh, and the other Tuatha De Danann, in both poetry and prose and did much to help spread their popularity although his depictions were more concerned with evocative descriptions than passing on genuine folklore. The Lugh of Yeats was a more romantic figure and one intrinsically linked to the sun. This reflected Yeats own personal approach to deity as expressions of moods or imagination (Williams, 2016). From this view gods become a way to convey wider themes in a poetic work or embody the desired mood or atmosphere of the text. Yeats also did much to shift the existing understanding of the sidhe as a numberless multitude into the commonly listed pantheon of Tuatha De Danann we find in books today (Williams, 2016).

Augusta Gregory, Gods and Fighting Men, 1904 – Lady Gregory may represent the first example of widely read re-telling of myths, where the core of the older mythology or story is retold in a new and partially fictionalized way. Her work was popular and has gained popularity again today, possible because it is easily accessed free online. This may present a challenge for readers that are new to Irish myth because her writing often combines multiple conflicting versions of tales, as well as her own ideas, into one whole that is presented in a way that may seem like genuinely older material.

Her writing is too extensive to recap fully here but for example her chapter 'The Coming of Lugh' combines material from the Lebor Gabala Erenn, Cath Maige Tuired, and Oidheadh Chloinne Tuireann along with her own flourishes into a single story the like of which had not existed previous to her writing it. She places Lugh in a central position throughout the story, repeatedly emphasizing his prophesied importance in driving out the Fomorians. For a second example in her chapter 'The Hidden House of Lugh' she retells the Baile and Scáil, but she adds material where Lugh is speaking to Conn so that she related his prophecy which is not found in the older text and she doesn't have Lugh stating that he is a dead human, but rather at the very end of the text has him simply declare himself 'Lugh son of Ethniu'.

Ella Young, Celtic Wonder Tales, 1910 – Ella Young was born in Ireland and emigrated later in life to California, USA. Considered an expert in Irish mythology she toured various universities and taught Celtic studies at Berkley. Despite this expertise her book 'Celtic Wonder Tales' takes extreme liberties with the older mythology, rewriting stories completely in places and creating new material in others. Her 'Celtic Wonder Tales' has become a common resource in the past hundred years and is enjoyed for its poetic text and evocative descriptions.

In Young's work we first meet Lugh in a story titled 'The Coming of Lugh' which retells the Cath Maige Tuired in parts but with alterations. Young's version begins with Manannan taking the child Lugh, who she calls a Sun God, away with him into Fairy from Ireland. She describes a variety of animals including lions, panthers, and unicorns that keep Lugh company as he grows. While he is with Manannan the Fomorians come to Ireland and steal the Dagda's cauldron and the spear (another of the treasures) leaving only the stone of Fál which prevents the Fomorians from fully taking over. Finally, Lugh reaches his 21st birthday and Manannan makes a show of giving him a gift, the sword[1] which is the fourth treasure and which has been in Manannan's keeping. When he touches it, Lugh remembers Ireland and pledges to go back. To help him Manannan equips him with a horse and armour. Lugh returns with a fairy host to Ireland, passing invisibly thanks to Manannan's magic until he reaches Nuada's court. He requests entry and is denied until he lists all his skills after which he is allowed in, then he best Ogma in a test of strength and plays chess. Finally, Nuada proclaims him 'Ildana' and Lugh plays music on the Dagda's harp which, according to Young, causes the seasons to turn. He lulls the court to sleep and slips away.

Lugh's presence inspired the Tuatha De to rebel and they go to Uisneach. A battle is about to begin when Lugh and the fairy host appear, Young comparing his approach to the rising of the sun. The Fomorians are destroyed save nine men who Lugh sends back to Balor to tell him and the other Fomorians that the De Danann are free from their oppression.

Lugh shows the Tuatha De Danann the sword and asks them for the other three treasures which they admit have been lost except for the stone. He then has them all swear an oath with the earth of Ireland on the sword and stone to fight and destroy the Fomorians. Shortly after this his father is killed by the sons of Tuireann and the earth sends a wind to tell Lugh. Lugh finds his father's body and gets the tale of his death, then goes to the assembly and accuses the sons of Tuireann who Nuada orders killed. Lugh stays his hand however and asks instead that they gain items useful in the upcoming battle. They agree to these terms and set off to acquire the list of items Lugh requests[2] engaging in adventures for each one. The three gain many of the treasures and Lugh, aware that they only have two left, decides they are succeeding too easily and puts a spell of forgetfulness on them so that they return early, however he immediately regrets this and sends out a second spell so that if the feel badly for what they have done they will not forget. They have no regret so they return early and are sent out a second time to gain the last two items. They manage to do this but are mortally wounded in the process. Finally, dying, they return to Ireland to give Lugh the items they have gained. Tuireann begs Lugh to heal his sons with the healing skin and so Lugh gives them the choice to be healed or to pass to the next life; they choose to go to the next life[3].

Next Young retells a version of the battle between the Tuatha De Danann and the Fomorians. The two groups meet and fight but Lugh stays back waiting for Balor who he believes will not enter the fight until later. A few days pass before Balor does appear and then Lugh and he have their epic confrontation. The two meet in a scene that describes the clash of darkness and light, with Lugh throwing the spear into Balor's eye and Balor dissolving into shadow.

This summarizes Young's stories about Lugh, which hopefully the reader can hold in contrast to the Irish mythology discussed in chapter 2. Young's Lugh is devoid of the fierce and tempestuous nature of the mythical Lugh and presented instead as a figure of light – figurative and literal – who acts as a saviour figure to the Tuatha De Danann.

Peter Berresford Ellis, Celtic Myth and Legend, 1989 – Ellis is an English historian and novelist who has written nearly 100 books, including several on Celtic mythology. 'Celtic Myth and Legend' is his attempt at retelling various famous myths from the Celtic language speaking cultures and includes a creation myth of the author's own imagination.

The book begins with a chapter titles 'The Ever Living Ones' that combines Ellis's own fictional creation story with a retelling of the Cath Maige Tuired. As with Young, Ellis takes creative liberties with the mythological material, for example attributing the sword to Lugh (not the spear which he gives to no one) and giving Lugh's lineage as an odd combination of the possible fathers we find in mythology, saying that he was the son of Cian who was the son of Cainte. In Ellis's version Lugh was kept from the battle of Maigh Tuired because the De Danann saw him as too valuable to risk and said *"his was the wisdom needed to serve humankind"* (Ellis, 1989 p 31). He also explains Nuada placing Lugh in charge for thirteen days as a means for Lugh to share his wisdom with them, before they set nine warriors to guard him from the battle. When Nuada was killed in the battle Lugh escaped and set out to join the fight, his arrival appearing like the sun's rising to the Fomorians. Lugh kills Balor with his sling and then leads the Tuatha De Danann to victory.

Ellis ends that section of text with a passage claiming that Lugh was reduced into the folkloric Leprechaun and that is how his fame and memory have been preserved. We will discuss this assertion separately later in this chapter, but suffice to say here that it is less than accurate.

Ellis goes on in the following chapters to retell several other Irish myths, including the Oidheadh Chloinne Tuireann with more accuracy. Although these retellings are written in a more exuberant manner than the originals and include expanded conversations the main themes and characters are kept relatively true to form. In itself this is good, but combined with the imaginative and less accurate earlier chapter this can be very misleading to readers who may struggle to sort out the accurate from the imaginative.

Mass Media Depictions

Besides the sources listed above which seek to retell folklore in some manner, the Irish gods have a penchant for showing up across an array of modern fiction and gaming material. These depictions are sometimes done well and other times seem to only take the name of a deity for a character which is otherwise unrecognizable. I am listing as many of these appearances by Lugh that I am aware of without any judgment as to the quality of the depiction.

Books

Kenneth Flint's 1980's Sidhe trilogy features some of Lugh's story retold in a fictional format.

In 'The Tapestry' series by Henry Neff, Lugh is the father of one of the characters.

Lugh is mentioned in several books of the 1990's Young Wizards series by Diane Duane. He is one of the powers that be and is incarnated as an avatar within first a macaw and then a wizard.

The 80's and 90's David Sullivan series by Tom Deitz has Lugh in the role of lord of Tir na nOg.

Games

In the 2002 game 'Fire Emblem: Binding Blade', a game set in a world of humans and dragons, there is a character named Lugh.

In the 2004 video game 'The Bard's Tale', Lugh is one of three monstrous guardians that the player must defeat. The game features references to real locations in Ireland and the Orkney Isles and touches on mythology and folklore, although in a heavily fictionalized way.

In the 2004 online role-playing game 'Mabinogi', Lugh is the name of one non-playable human character. The game, like others, is heavily based on Celtic mythology and uses modified Irish language names for places, as well as Irish and Welsh names for times of year.

In the 2012 role-playing video game 'Devil Survivor 2', the

essence of Lugh is required to activate the Dragon Stream, a necessary step for the character being payed.

Lugh also is listed as one possible god a character can worship in some versions of Dungeons and Dragons

Television

In the 1990s series 'Mystic Knights of Tir Na Nog' Lugh is mentioned as a deity worshipped by the characters of the show.

The 'American Gods' TV show suggested at one point that the character of Mad Sweeney may be an incarnated form of the god Lugh, although the character himself refutes this.

Art

Another important way that Lugh exists in modern terms is through artwork. We have no known historic depictions from Ireland of Lugh but he appears in modern artwork across both Irish sources and pagan ones. Because of the lack of historic references these are highly personal interpretations which can vary widely, from the sculptural image created by Paul Borda of Dryad Design which shows Lugh sitting within a ring of solar fire to the imagery of Jane Brideson which shows Lugh as a dark-haired man holding a spear. For those that like art with a more classic feel to it George Russell, in the late 19th and early 20th centuries, painted images of the sidhe and figures including Lugh.

Lugh also appears in music, particularly modern folk and pagan music, as do mentions of him in songs about Lúnasa. Some examples include:

Kellianna – Lugh
Omnia – Lughnasadh
Damh the Bard – Lughnasadh
Emerald Rose – Before the Twilight Falls (about Lleu Llaw Gyffes)

Leprechauns

It's a very popular folk etymology to say that the word Leprechaun comes from 'little Lugh' or that Leprechauns are modern diminished versions of the older pagan deity Lugh. This concept will even appear in older academic texts.

This is fallacious however, so I think it's important to tackle it here. The word Leprechaun is a borrowing into older Irish as Luchropán from Latin, possibly related to Lupercus; it was previously broken down as lú = small / corp = body / án= diminutive term giving us a 'small bodied one' (Quinn, 1983; eDIL, 2018). Leprechauns appear in stories including the Echtra Fergusso Meic Leiti and Aided Fergusso Meic Leidi which date back concurrently with stories of the Tuatha De Danann, including Lugh, making it difficult to support the idea that they would represent a diminished form of the God. In these stories, leprechauns are very different from the modern conception, being small water sprites organized into a kingdom; they are dangerous beings with power to kill or destroy.

Modern Paganism

Lugh has a strong place in modern paganism, particularly any paganism that favours Celtic or Irish deities. Because he has been so thoroughly equated with the sun in some modern sources and because its common in neopagan witchcraft to pair sun and moon deities he has also gained some popularity there. He may be especially honoured by musicians or poets and is often acknowledged as a versatile deity of all skills, and therefore one that can be contacted for numerous purposes.

This is only a quick overview of Lugh in the modern world. Those seeking to go deeper with this can try reading modern books on Celtic paganism or Celtic Gods to get a more thorough idea of how Lugh is understood and related to today. His character and personality has diverged from the older stories, mellowing somewhat and losing some of the fierceness that marked the original Lugh. While many aspects of the older pagan deity have been lost in the modern perception of him his major facets have been retained, particularly his connections to skill and warriorship. And as has been thoroughly discussed he has found a place as a sun deity for many people.

End Notes

1   Young's version is almost entirely at odds with actual mythology including who she attributes the sword and spear to at various points and how she explains the reasons for events occurring. I'm also concerned with the way she characterizes the Tuatha De as shining and good and the Fomorians as ugly and malformed, which at the least is a mischaracterization of the Fomorians some of whom were quite beautiful. Because of these things I highly recommend people read Young's work with a larger than normal grain of salt.

2   Here would be Young's retelling of the Oidheadh Chloinne Tuireann, although as with everything else much altered. The items are largely the same but Lugh's motivation is much purer, based in aiding the Tuatha De more generally and it is Tuireann himself who goes to Lugh to ask for the loan of Manannan's boat when his sons refuse to ask any help of Lugh. Lugh shows no great enmity – or any enmity at all – towards his father's killers and the fine he asks is not a clever deception to get them killed and he does offer them healing in the end of Young's tale rather than refusing it. All of this casts Lugh in a profoundly different light (pun intended) than the original mythology.

3   There are some very heavy-handed Christian overtones in this section, with Lugh asking the brothers if they want 'the king's robe or the beggar's cloak' to which they reply they do not want the beggar's cloak, that is life (Young, 1910). The final passage takes place in Young's 'Tir na Moe' or land of

the living where we see the already deceased Cian warmly greeting the Sons of Tuireann and the four acting as friends and comrades.

Chapter 6

Connecting to Lugh

"The Gods have returned to Erin and have centred themselves in the sacred mountains and blow the fires through the country. They have been seen by several in vision, they will awaken the magical instinct everywhere and the universal heart of the people will turn to the old...beliefs." George Russell, 1896

Having hopefully gained a basic understanding of who Lugh is and what he is associated with, the next step, if you choose to, is to work to actively connect to him as a deity. There is no right or wrong in doing this but in this chapter I will offer some suggestions for ways that I have found to be effective. These are only suggestions and should not be viewed as rigid rules; one key to this sort of thing is to find out what works best for you as an individual and focus on that rather than trying to force yourself to connect through a process that may not speak to you.

Communication

A common question that people ask when first beginning to establish a relationship with a deity is how that deity may communicate with them. Humans communicate regularly with deity through prayer but how can we perceive the other end of that conversation? This will of course vary somewhat depending on the deity but I will offer some basic suggestions that you can try out.

Dreams: one of the most common ways that people find themselves – voluntarily or otherwise – communicating with deities is in dreams. These may be obvious dreams where a deity appears to you and talks or more obscure dreams where you feel like it is connected to the deity but aren't always sure how. A good idea is to keep a dream journal so you can look for patterns or record more obvious interactions. Just remember that interactions in dreams have as much weight as interactions while awake.

Divination – if you are unsure of your own ability to discern messages or to receive them then one option is to go to someone else who is skilled with divination and ask them to intercede for you[1].

Omens – Omens are naturally occurring things in the world around you that you may find have special significance. These are things that are unusual or uncommon or that happen at a specific time and will usually have personal significance. There are also systems of omens that can be found within cultures. I recommend omens as one way to communicate with Lugh but you may have to create your own system which can be a slow process. Ask a question and then wait to see what happens, if anything. Keep notes and look for patterns.

Meditation – possibly the most direct method would be to seek the deity out during meditation or journeywork. This allows for conversation in many cases and for the person to ask questions and potentially get direct answers.

It is important when dealing with this method of communication to be especially discerning of any information gained in the meditation and to focus on one's self within the framework. Messages in meditation fall into the realm of personal gnosis and while they can be very powerful, they shouldn't be projected out onto other people or directed to communities or groups.

Creating an Altar

Altars will always be highly personal affairs but if you are seeking to use an altar or shrine to connect to Lugh, I will offer some suggestions. As with other Irish deities there are multiple ways to approach this because Lugh is a deity with many different facets. Below I will offer a variety of options based on specific aspects of Lugh one might wish to connect to, as well as a more general one.

In general terms many altars tend to include a focal point such as an image, statue, or symbol of the deity. It is entirely up to the reader whether or not you wish to include an image[2] of Lugh himself or not; alternatives would include a stone or item to represent him instead.

Lugh as king – One of Lugh's main aspects is Lugh as king of the Tuatha De Danann or as a mediator of sovereignty. If you wish to connect to this particular energy

Lugh as healer – In the story of Lugh and Cu Chulainn during the Táin Bó Cúailnge Lugh acts as a healer for his son, using herbs and charms to heal Cu Chulainn's battle wounds and exhaustion. He also declares himself a physician when requesting entry into Teamhair during the Cath Maige Tuired. While this is not a widely acknowledged aspect of Lugh if you find that you would like to connect to Lugh as healer, I would suggest making an altar focused around that. You could use a green cloth and place a mortar and pestle on it, perhaps with some fresh or dried herbs.

Lugh as musician or poet – To represent Lugh as a musician or poet I suggest items associated with those arts in Ireland, such as a harp, or books of poetry, history, or music. If you yourself are a musician you might also include your own instrument or something representing it in the space.

Lugh as warrior – To create a space for Lugh as a warrior you might want to use a leather altar cloth or one in red. An image of him (if you choose to include it) should be one with a more martial tone, perhaps including him brandishing his spear or prepared for battle. Symbolic weaponry like a spear, sword, or sling might also be used.

Lugh as master of skill –Lugh lists a variety of arts that he is able to practice in the Cath Maige Tuired when he is requesting entrance into Teamhair. For those seeking to fashion an altar to Lugh as the master of all skills it can be beneficial to look to this list for ideas of items to include or focus on. For example, Lugh mentions being a cupbearer so a cup might be included. He also says he is a smith and brazier so you could choose to incorporate tools associated with this like a hammer, anvil, tongs, or even wrought iron pieces.

Lugh – If you want to have an altar that focuses on Lugh in a more general way there are two directions you can go in. You can create a space that includes symbols or items associated with all of the various skills that Lugh is connected to or you can make a very simple space for him. If you decide on the first option then perhaps you could use various small images that remind you of Lugh's various purviews or try to find items representing them, such as a crown, spear, chariot, herbs, harp, chess board or reconstructed fidchell board, lightning, a sling or round stone (for a sling stone), or a dog/hound.

Offerings

We have no historic records of what may have been offered to Lugh during the pagan period, however we can look to later folklore and folk practices for ideas as well as at what modern pagans have been doing. By these accounts, offerings might include poetry, athletic feats, grain, bread, ale or beer, mead, or milk (a long-standing traditional offering to any of the Gods or people of the sidhe). Additionally, any harvest foods, like berries, are also good offerings for him.

Prayers to Lugh

I strongly encourage readers who are interested in praying

to Lugh to fashion their own prayers; these will always have more power. That said though I know that people sometimes feel uncertain about doing that especially early on and also that some people just prefer to use prewritten prayers. To that end I am going to offer a selection of prayers here that people can utilize if they choose to. Pronouns can be changed as needed.

Invocation to Lugh
I call upon Lugh
The many skilled
The spear-furious
The sun-faced
Great king of the Gods
Who led the Tuatha De to victory
Who vanquished mighty Balor
May you be with us now
May you bless us as we honour you
May you receive our offerings
Lugh, son of Cian
Lugh son of Ethniu
Lugh of the long arm
Be with us now!

Prayer to The God of Skill
Lugh Ildanach
Lugh Samildanach
God of many skills
Master of all arts
Help me now to find
My own skill
Help me to succeed
In the task before me
Help me to master
The art I seek to practice

Lugh, god of all talents,
Hear my prayer
Receive my offering
Bring me your wisdom

Musicians Prayer to Lugh
I call to Lugh, poet and harper,
Who plays the three strains:
For sleep
For sorrow
For joy
Lugh Ildanach
May I be inspired
May my music be true
May it speak to my audience
I ask this of you
As a musician, a child of art,
May your power find me

Prayer to Lugh for Protection
Lugh Lonnbeimnech
Warrior of the Tuatha
Whose skill turned the battle
Who drove out oppressors
Who freed his kin
Lugh of the spear and sling
We ask for your protection
And your aid as we
Seek to protect ourselves
May your swift spear defend us
May your cloak be between
Us and all harm
Lugh Lonnsclech
Let it be so

Meditation to Meet Lugh

A guided meditation can be a good way to start to reach out to a deity and I recommend them as a good first step to active connection. Even if you have limited or no experience with meditation, it's fairly simple to do and should be safe. You can memorize the meditation script and then run through it yourself, record yourself reading it and then play it back while meditating, or have a friend read it to you. If you want to do this meditation just find a quiet time and place, sit or lay comfortably, and run through the script I'll include below.

It doesn't have to be done perfectly and you should try to be open to the possibility of things going a bit off script: you may have no experience at all and need to do the meditation several times or you might find that your actual experience in the meditation doesn't follow the pre-written story. That's fine. The only thing you should watch for is anything coming up in the meditation that is upsetting or frightening. If at any time you feel unsafe or want to stop you can picture a door appearing in front of you and see yourself opening it and immediately being back in your own body and awake.

To do the meditation make sure you have enough time undisturbed. Get into a comfortable position and begin.

Relax and feel the ground below you. Feel yourself solid on the earth. Breath in slowly. Breath out. In. And out. See yourself surrounded by bright white light and know that you are perfectly safe and protected. Breath in slowly and deeply and feel the light filling you. Breath out.

The white light starts to fade around you and you become aware that you are sitting on a green hillside. The sky is blue above you. The air is warm and there is a slight, gentle breeze against your skin. You can hear birds in the distance and the subtle sound of animals.

Look around you and make note of what you are seeing. Are there stones on the hillside with you? A cairn? Is there water nearby or trees? Let yourself feel the sun and wind as you relax into the space. This is a peaceful place and you sit and enjoy the feel of the warm earth beneath.

After a time, you glance up and see a figure moving towards you across the green grass. It is a man, his curling blond hair held back by a crown. He is wearing a green tunic with a silver belt and sword, a darker green cloak fringed in gold around his shoulders. He is walking easily up the incline of the hill and when he sees you watching him, he smiles at you. His expression is thoughtful and curious. You recognize him as Lugh of the Long-Arm, the many skilled King of the Tuatha De Danann.

He walks up until he is standing near you and he also takes a moment to breathe deeply, seeming to enjoy the energy of this place. After a moment he greets you by name and then offers you a hand up so that you are standing next to him. As you stand together you have the opportunity to tell him anything you want to or ask him questions and he gives you any messages he has for you (leave time here for discussion).

When all has been said that needs to be said Lugh steps away, in the direction he came from. As he turns to leave, he reminds you that you may always seek his presence at this hill, although he makes no promises that he will always be free to appear. Then with a final nod he gestures and a fine-looking horse emerges from the air to stand at the near him. He mounts easily and the pair turn and move away, quickly disappearing from sight.

You sit for another moment, breathing deeply the scent of grass and sunshine, then you prepare to leave as well. You sit back down in the spot you first arrived at. All you see around you is green hill and blue sky. The sun is warm and the breeze is cool and you feel peaceful and content. Closing your eyes, the green fades and then is consumed by white light which gets brighter and brighter.

Breath in slowly. Breath out. Again. Feel the earth solidly beneath you. Feel yourself solidly within your own body. Breath in.

Out. Shift your weight, move your body, wiggle fingers and toes.
When you feel ready open your eyes.

After the meditation write down any experiences you have had.

Lugh is still a powerful force in the modern world and has been steadily gaining in popularity in pagan communities. The Lugh of today is anchored in the Lugh of the past but has also been altered in significant ways, for example now being seen strongly as a sun god. As we seek to move forward and find our own connection to Lugh, we can use all of the mythology and stories of Lugh as a foundation, but we must also actively seek him out. All of the things suggested in this chapter are just that, suggestions. They can be helpful tools to get you started but they are only tools and have as much value as you give them. And like any tools in spirituality what works for some people will not work for others so as you move forward, I encourage you to experiment and find what works best for you.

End Notes

1   It is possible to preform divination for yourself however I generally don't advise it, particularly if you are only just beginning with either divination or your relationship with a particular deity. It is too easy to mislead yourself and see what you want or what you fear.

2   We have no surviving images of Lugh from Ireland and limited evidence of his imagery elsewhere. There is also a debate about whether or not the historic Celtic cultures used imagery of their Gods at all or if they practiced an aniconic religion. Some modern pagans feel very strongly that the historic Celts didn't use imagery and that modern Celtic-based pagans should not either while others disagree and feel that the use of such imagery is in line with similar practices by closely related pagan cultures, such as the Norse. Ultimately it is a personal decision.

Conclusion

Lugh is a multi-faceted and multi-skilled deity who is well known even today among many pagans. His mythology is complex and shows us a deity who is bold and powerful, but also stubborn and sometimes unforgiving. He was a successful king to the Tuatha De Danann, and in the story of Baile an Scáil he appears alongside the personification of sovereignty, speaking to the one who would be the human king of Ireland. And in later folklore before being displaced by saint Patrick it was Lugh who secured the harvest by contesting against Crom Cruach, reinforcing his role as a God who supports the proper order of civilization. There are certainly many things in Lugh that a modern pagan might choose to connect to or honour.

It speaks to the essential importance of Lugh and the way that the core of his stories have remained relevant that he is still a force today, celebrated in song and art. An ancient deity under various names who has been honoured in Gaul, Ireland, and Wales and who is now known across the world. There is something intrinsic to Lugh and his mythology that stays with people and inspires them to continue dreaming of the many skilled king. Something in him that will always speak to something in us.

Despite all of the sources we have that discuss him the truth of who and what Lugh is cannot be easily disambiguated. His parentage is clearly laid out and full of contradictions. Who fostered him is listed in many sources yet the lists rarely agree. He has existed across myth and folklore as a god and as a person of the fairy hills, as a 'scál' and as a human ancestor. He has been a god of storms and lightning and is now often seen as a god of the sun. He has been a king and a mediator of sovereignty. The older mythological Lugh was a fierce, quick tempered warrior while the later modern depiction shifted into an almost Christ-like figure. All of these are Lugh and in all these contradictions we find wholeness.

This book has been only a small and brief introduction to the depth that is found in studying Lugh. I strongly encourage people who are interested in going deeper to keep digging, to read the myths and folklore for themselves. To embark on a quest to uncover the entirety of who Lugh is which is far too much to ever include in such a humble book as this. This is only the first small glimpse into the immensity of Lugh.

Keep looking.

Appendix A – Story Names and Terms

I am often asked to include a pronunciation guide in my books as well as a guide to the English names for the Irish myths. I have made a personal commitment myself to use Irish names for people, places, and stories as often as possible because I feel this is both important and in line with the way many other cultures are treated respectfully. Below I will include a glossary of the names of the myths in the Irish, as I include them throughout this book, followed by the most common English name for the same story as well as a short list of important terms and their meanings.

Glossary of Story Names

Compert Con Culainn – The Birth of Cu Chulainn
Lebor Gabala Erenn – The Book of the Takings of Ireland
Cath Maige Tuired – Battle of the Plain of Pillars
Cét Cath Maige Tuired – First Battle of the Plain of Pillars
Baile na Scáil – Vision of the Phantom
Oidheadh Chloinne Tuireann – Fate of the Children of Tuireann
Tuatha De Danand na Set Soim – the Treasures of the Tuatha De Danann
Táin Bó Cúailnge – The Cattle Raid of Cooley
Dindshenchas – place name stories
Gabail an t-Side – The Taking of the Sidhe
Tochmarc Emire – Wooing of Emer
Acallamh na Senorach – Conversation of the Sages

Terms/Places

Brugh – home, hall, palace
Eamhain Abhlac – Place of Apples, a name for the Otherworldly island ruled by Manannán
Sidhe – a fairy hill or mound; by extension used for the inhabitants

of the fairy hills as well

Oenach – modern Irish aonach, a harvest fair

Teamhair – Tara, co Meath

Cairn ui Neit – Mizen Head, co Cork

Maigh Tuired – 'plain of pillars', anglicized as Moytirra, located in Sligo

Appendix B – Pronunciation Guide

This is a small section with some of the deity names and other Irish language names or terms included in the book and how they would be pronounced in modern Irish. While I do have some modern Irish myself my main focus is older Irish so I recommend treating this as a rough guideline not a definitive guide; also keep in mind there are dialect variations so that, for example, Badb is Byve in some places and Bow in others.

Abridged Pronunciation Guide
Aengus – Ayn-guhs
Áine – Awn-yuh
Aoife – Ee-fuh
Badb – Byve
Bodb Derg – Bove Jehrg
Brugh - brew
Buí - Bwee
Cailleach – Kayl-yuck
Cethen – Keh-hen
Cian – Keen
Conchobar – Con-(ch)uh-vahr with the ch like in loch
Cu - Koo
Cu Chulainn – Koo (ch)ul-ahn with the ch like in loch
Dagda – Dahg-dah
Dian Cecht – Deen Keh-(ch)-t with the ch like in loch
Echtach – E(ch)-tahk
Emhain Abhlac – Ehw-ahn Av-lak
Enbhar – Ehn-var
Ethniu – Eh-noo
Fand – Fahnd with the a like in father
Féth fíadha – Fay Fee-ah
Fuamnach – Fuhmna(ch) with the ch like in loch

Laeg - Layg

Lugh – Loo

Macha – Mah-kah although the ch is swallowed a bit

Manannán – Mah-nah-nawn

Midhir – Me'er

Morrigan – More-ih-guhn

Mórríghain – More-ree-uhn (this is the modern Irish spelling and pronunciation)

Nás - Naws

Sidhe – shee

Tailltiu – Tall-tchew

Teamhair – Teh-war

Tír na nÓg – Teer nuh Nowg

Tír Tairngire – Teer Tahrn-gih-reh

Tuireann – Tuhr-ehn

Bibliography

Copeland Burlase, W., (1897) The Dolmens of Ireland: Their Distribution, Structural Characteristics, and Affinities in Other Countries; Together with the Folk-lore Attaching to Them; Supplemented by Considerations on the Anthropology, Ethnology, and Traditions of the Irish People. With Four Maps, and Eight Hundred Illustrations, Including Two Coloured Plates, Volume 3

Cross, T., and Slover, H., (1936) Ancient Irish Tales

Curtin, J., (1894) Hero-Tales of Ireland

Daimler, M., (2015) The Treasure of the Tuatha De Danann

--- (2017) Lugh's Arrival at Tara. Retrieved from https://lairbhan. blogspot.com/2017/07/poem-translation-lughs-arrival-at. html?m=1

Dillon, M., (1946) The Cycle of Kings

Dunn, E., (1913) Táin Bó Cualgne

eDIL (2020) Electronic Dictionary of the Irish Language. Retrieved from http://dil.ie/search?q=leprechaun

Evans-Wentz, W., (1911) The Fairy Faith in Celtic Countries

Gray, E., (1983) Cath Maige Tuired

Gregory, A., (1904) Gods and Fighting Men

Gwyn, E., (1913) Metrical Dindshenchas part III

--- (1924) Metrical Dindshenchas part IV

Hicks, R., (2012) 'The Lughnasa Triangle: Astronomical Symbolism in the Ancient Irish Sacred Landscape' Archeoastronomy. Retrieved from https://www.academia.edu/41221856/ The_Lughnasa_Triangle_Astronomical_Symbolism_in_the_ Ancient_Irish_Sacred_Landscape?fbclid=IwAR3bH454glxnQ plitZfNggxj9wwdBIAS_JkXee1H3XBOQ-hyxowHeREsnb4

Jones, M., (2020) The Birth of Cu Chulainn. Retrieved from https://www.maryjones.us/ctexts/cuchulain1.html

Koch, J., (1992) 'Further to tongu do dia toinges mo thuath ["Mi a dyngaf dynged it"]'; Études Celtiques 29 (1992) 249–6. Retrieved from https://www.academia.edu/7242277/Further_ to_tongu_do_dia_toinges_mo_thuath_Mi_a_dyngaf_ dynged_it_and_c

--- (2006) Celtic Culture: a historical encyclopaedia

Kondratiev, A., (1997) Lugh the Many Gifted Lord. Retrieved from http://www.imbas.org/articles/lugus.html

Macalister, R., (1941) Lebor Gabala Erenn

MacKillop, J., (1998) Dictionary of Celtic Mythology

MacNeill, E., (2015) Dunaire Finn, The Book of the Lays of Fionn, vol 1

McCone, K., (2000) Pagan Past and Christian Present in Early Irish Literature

McDevitte, W., and Bohn, W., (2012) The Gallic Wars

McGinley, S., Potito, A., Molloy, K., Schot, R., Stuijts, R., and Beilman, D., (2015) *Lough Lugh, Uisneach: from natural lake to archaeological monument?* The Journal of Irish Archaeology Vol. 24

McNeill, M., (1962) The Festival of Lughnasa

Meyer, K., (1888) *'The Wooing of Emer'* in Archaeological Review vol 1

Murphy, G., (1956) Early Irish Lyrics, Eighth to Twelfth Century

Parker, W., (2003) The Mabinogi of Math. Retrieved from http:// www.mabinogi.net/math.htm

O Cathasaigh, T., (2013) Coire Sois: The Cauldron of Knowledge a Companion to Early Irish Saga

O hOgain, D., (2006) The Lore of Ireland

O'Grady, S., (1892) Silva Gadelica

O'Rahilly, T., (1946) Early Irish History and Mythology

--- (1976) Táin Bó Cúailnge Recension 1

Quinn, E., (1983). Dictionary of the Irish Language: Based Mainly on Old and Middle Irish Materials

Sanas Cormaic (n.d.) Early Irish Glossaries Database. Retrieved from http://www.asnc.cam.ac.uk/irishglossaries/

Sims-Williams, P., (2011) Irish Influence on Medieval Welsh Literature

Sjoestedt, M., (2000) Celtic Gods and Heroes

Smyth, D., (1988) A Guide to Irish Mythology

Stokes, W., (1891) The Second Battle of Moytura

Waddell, J., (2014) Archaeology and Celtic Myth

Williams, M., (2016) Ireland's Immortals: A History of the Gods of Irish Myth

Young, E., (1910) Celtic Wonder Tales

**MOON
BOOKS**

PAGANISM & SHAMANISM

What is Paganism? A religion, a spirituality, an alternative belief system, nature worship? You can find support for all these definitions (and many more) in dictionaries, encyclopaedias, and text books of religion, but subscribe to any one and the truth will evade you. Above all Paganism is a creative pursuit, an encounter with reality, an exploration of meaning and an expression of the soul. Druids, Heathens, Wiccans and others, all contribute their insights and literary riches to the Pagan tradition. Moon Books invites you to begin or to deepen your own encounter, right here, right now. If you have enjoyed this book, why not tell other readers by posting a review on your preferred book site.

Recent bestsellers from Moon Books are:

Journey to the Dark Goddess
How to Return to Your Soul
Jane Meredith
Discover the powerful secrets of the Dark Goddess and
transform your depression, grief and pain into healing
and integration.
Paperback: 978-1-84694-677-6 ebook: 978-1-78099-223-5

Shamanic Reiki
Expanded Ways of Working with Universal Life Force Energy
Llyn Roberts, Robert Levy
Shamanism and Reiki are each powerful ways of healing; together,
their power multiplies. *Shamanic Reiki* introduces techniques to
help healers and Reiki practitioners tap ancient healing wisdom.
Paperback: 978-1-84694-037-8 ebook: 978-1-84694-650-9

Pagan Portals – The Awen Alone
Walking the Path of the Solitary Druid
Joanna van der Hoeven
An introductory guide for the solitary Druid, *The Awen Alone* will
accompany you as you explore, and seek out your own place
within the natural world.
Paperback: 978-1-78279-547-6 ebook: 978-1-78279-546-9

A Kitchen Witch's World of Magical Herbs & Plants
Rachel Patterson
A journey into the magical world of herbs and plants, filled with
magical uses, folklore, history and practical magic. By popular
writer, blogger and kitchen witch, Tansy Firedragon.
Paperback: 978-1-78279-621-3 ebook: 978-1-78279-620-6

Medicine for the Soul
The Complete Book of Shamanic Healing
Ross Heaven
All you will ever need to know about shamanic healing and how to
become your own shaman...
Paperback: 978-1-78099-419-2 ebook: 978-1-78099-420-8

Shaman Pathways – The Druid Shaman
Exploring the Celtic Otherworld
Danu Forest
A practical guide to Celtic shamanism with exercises and
techniques as well as traditional lore for exploring the Celtic
Otherworld.
Paperback: 978-1-78099-615-8 ebook: 978-1-78099-616-5

Traditional Witchcraft for the Woods and Forests
A Witch's Guide to the Woodland with Guided Meditations and
Pathworking
Mélusine Draco
A Witch's guide to walking alone in the woods, with guided
meditations and pathworking.
Paperback: 978-1-84694-803-9 ebook: 978-1-84694-804-6

Naming the Goddess
Trevor Greenfield
Naming the Goddess is written by over eighty adherents and
scholars of Goddess and Goddess Spirituality.
Paperback: 978-1-78279-476-9 ebook: 978-1-78279-475-2

Shapeshifting into Higher Consciousness
Heal and Transform Yourself and Our World with Ancient
Shamanic and Modern Methods
Llyn Roberts
Ancient and modern methods that you can use every day to
transform yourself and make a positive difference in the world.
Paperback: 978-1-84694-843-5 ebook: 978-1-84694-844-2

Readers of ebooks can buy or view any of these bestsellers by
clicking on the live link in the title. Most titles are published in
paperback and as an ebook. Paperbacks are available in traditional
bookshops. Both print and ebook formats are available online.

Find more titles and sign up to our readers' newsletter at
http://www.johnhuntpublishing.com/paganism
Follow us on Facebook at https://www.facebook.com/MoonBooks
and Twitter at https://twitter.com/MoonBooksJHP

Other Irish mythology titles from Morgan Daimler

Brigid

Meeting the Celtic Goddess of Poetry, Forge, and Healing Well

978-1-78535-320-8 (Paperback)
978-1-78535-321-5 (e-book)

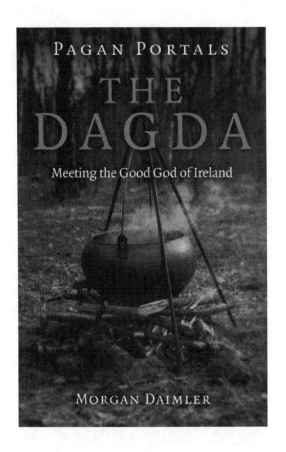

The Dagda

Meeting the Good God of Ireland

978-1-78535-640-7 (Paperback)
978-1-78535-641-4 (e-book)

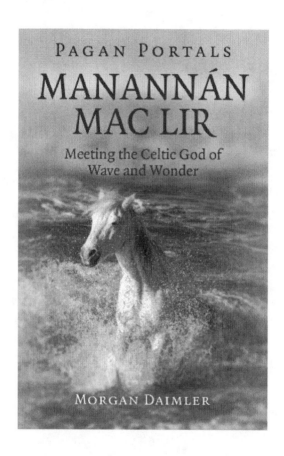

Manannán mac Lir

Meeting the Celtic God of Wave and Wonder

978-1-78535-810-4 (Paperback)
978-1-78535-811-1 (e-book)

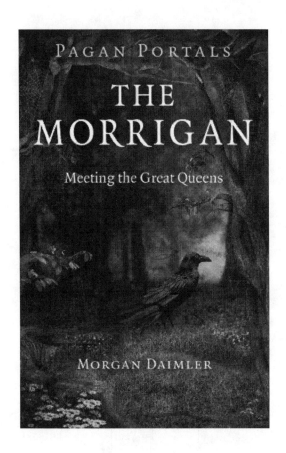

The Morrigan

Meeting the Great Queens

978-1-78279-833-0 (Paperback)
978-1-78279-834-7 (e-book)

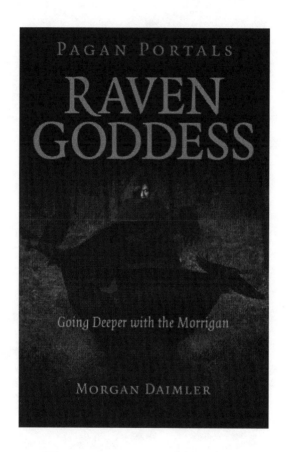

Raven Goddess

Going Deeper with the Morrigan

978-1-78904-486-7 (Paperback)
978-1-78904-487-4 (e-book)

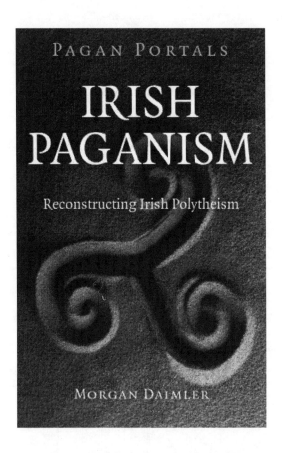

Irish Paganism

Reconstructing Irish Polytheism

978-1-78535-145-7 (Paperback)
978-1-78535-146-4 (e-book)